Praise for

DEEPER, *Richer*, FULLER

"It is with delight that I congratulate my longtime friend and colleague Tom Paterson on completion of his spiritual magnum opus. For nearly forty years, I have been a witness of the sojourn that Tom so openly and passionately shares with the reader. Having lectured alongside him in a UCLA management seminar in Mexico City, studied him in executive sessions in Palm Springs, and walked the Great Wall in China with him, I can confirm that God has done a remarkable and continuing rework in Tom that attests to his own Deeper, Richer, Fuller spiritual life. He knows firsthand of what he writes!"

—Vernon L. Grose, DSc; chairman,
Omega Systems Group Incorporated

"Through Tom's many life experiences and life challenges, Tom has achieved what many of us long for—a personal close relationship with the God of the universe. With this *Deeper, Richer, Fuller* book, Tom shares with us the strategic and simple steps he calls LifeGates to help us get us there."

—Jerry Kehe, chairman of the board,
Kehe Food Distributors

"Tom Paterson has been gifted by God with a unique and special understanding of full surrender of one's entire being to the Lord. He in turn has shared this gift with us in *Deeper, Richer, Fuller*. He relates his personal story, his journey from being a Christian in name only to a complete surrender, with an interactive writing style that draws the reader in personally and shares not only the what but also the how for all who love God and seek eternal life. Regardless of age, profession, religion, or spiritual status, every reader will praise God and Tom for the gift of these insights."

—Gary E. Liebl, chairman emeritus,
Chaminade University of Honolulu

"Tom Patterson is a master at conceiving and developing processes. Tom cogently refines the process that can lead the reader to a Christ-centered life. As you will discover, it is a process inspired by the Holy Spirit. It describes a journey that is well worth the effort and can lead you to a deeper, richer, fuller life."

—L. David Black, former chairman, president, and CEO
of JLG Industries, San Antonio, Texas

DEEPER, *Richer*, **FULLER**

DEEPER,
Richer,
FULLER

Discover the Spiritual Life You Long For

TOM PATERSON

HOWARD BOOKS
A DIVISION OF SIMON & SCHUSTER, INC.
New York · Nashville · London · Toronto · Sydney

Published by Howard Books, a division of Simon & Schuster, Inc.
1230 Avenue of the Americas, New York, NY 10020

Deeper, Richer, Fuller copyright © 2010 Tom Paterson

In association with the literary agency of "Bucky" Richard Rosenbaum, Rosenbaum Literary Agency.

Library of Congress Cataloging-in-Publication Data

Paterson, Tom.
Deeper, richer, fuller : discover the spiritual life you long for / Tom Paterson.
p. cm.
1. Christian life. 2. Spiritual life—Christianity. I. Title.
BV4501.3.P38 2010
248.4—dc22   2010008482

ISBN 978-1-4391-3569-3
ISBN 978-1-4391-5537-0 (ebook)
10 9 8 7 6 5 4 3 2 1

For information regarding special discounts for bulk purchases,
please contact: Simon & Schuster Special Sales at 1-866-506-1949 or
business@simonandschuster.com.

The Simon & Schuster Speakers Bureau can bring authors to your live event. For more information or to book an event, contact the Simon & Schuster Speakers Bureau at 1-866-248-3049 or visit our website at www.simonspeakers.com.

CONTENTS

In the beginning was the Word,
and the Word was with God,
and the Word was God. . . .
He was in the world and the
world was made through Him,
and the world did not know Him.
He came to His own,
and those who were His own did not receive Him.
But as many as received Him,
to them He gave the right
to become children of God,
even to those who believe in His name,
who were born, not of blood
nor of the will of the flesh,
nor of the will of man, but of God.
And the Word became flesh and dwelt among us,
and we beheld His glory,
glory as of the only begotten of the Father,
full of grace and truth.

—JOHN 1:1, 10–14

Abba is the diminutive form of an Aramaic word for God the Father. It literally means "Daddy." The word came to us from God through His Son, Christ Jesus, Who taught us that our Father wants a loving, close "Daddy" relationship with each of His children.

This book is reverently dedicated to Abba.

Introduction

To Fully Live, Live a Life of Love

I once planned to ask God for a special grace when the time to go home was upon me: "Give me a few moments more to enjoy a baby's smile . . . the laughter of a child . . . the love of my family . . . the warmth of treasured friendships. And to tell you, Lord, how grateful I am for You in my life . . . for my beautiful country, my family, and my life."

God replied in a gentle voice: "I have a better idea, my child. Take these moments now. Take them fully, making them a part of your everyday life. Living the life I shaped you for is all about love—My love. I'm in that baby's smile. You can hear me in the glorious laughter of a child. You can feel My love in the love of family members one for another. The warmth of old friendships is My love. I know you are mine, but your busyness keeps you half alive. Let yourself feel My presence, My love, in everything around you. You'll get a sense of what lies ahead. You will become radiantly alive. This is my dream for you. This will give Me great joy."

With a full and trembling heart I made a solemn commitment: "I will live Your dream for me: a life of love—Your love: sensing, receiving, sharing, and giving it."

I've had my share of love in my life. I was married to a wonderful woman for fifty-four years, Ginny, and then, when Ginny was gone, was blessed to find love with another woman, Meryl, with whom I shared my life for another five years. I've enjoyed the love of children, and that of many friends. But it is in discovering the deepest, richest, fullest love possible—God's love—and an active, interactive relationship with Him, that I've come to know what life is all about.

His dream for me—to sense, receive, and share His love in and out of every hour of my life—is also His dream for you. And I'm here to tell you, it is possible. Come, let's explore what I call our "LifeGates," and discover where we are on the journey, and how we might get one step further toward a *deeper, richer, fuller* life with God. Because a relationship with God is not something one attains—it's something you're already a part of (whether you realize it or not).

DEEPER, *Richer*, FULLER

chapter 1

The Invitation to Friendship

J*esus was very clear on* what it takes to be His friend:

> *"You are my friends if you do whatever I command you."*
>
> —JOHN 15:14

And He commands us to love one another:

> *"This is My commandment, that you love one another as I have loved you."*
>
> —JOHN 15:12

But we cannot do what pleases God apart from Him:

> *"I am the vine, you are the branches. He who abides in Me, and I in him, bears much fruit; for without Me you can do nothing."*
>
> —JOHN 15:5

To live with Jesus in us, to do what He commands and understand what pleases Him, we must be awakened believers, not asleep. Jesus spoke the words above as He was getting ready to go home. He was giving instructions to His disciples on how to live a full, joyous life; a life lived to the full here . . . not the counterfeit life of one asleep to our Lord.

> *"These things I have spoken to you, that My joy may remain in you and that your joy may be full."*
>
> —JOHN 15:11

I couldn't always hear God's voice. I was a workaholic, working six long days a week and sleeping in on Sunday mornings. Sunday afternoons, I tended my garden. I was too busy to hear His voice. I was a "casual" Christian for the first twenty years of my marriage. Most of the time it was my wife who took our children to Sunday School while she attended church alone. It wasn't until our young daughter Debbie fell ill with spinal cancer that I woke up. I was trying to live a moral, honest life alone. I know about being asleep. That was me. During this period, there were a few years where I taught a Sunday School class. I attended a couples club at our church. I was doing all the right things, on a surface level. And yet I was a seeker without knowing it. And God was seeking me.

When Debbie fell ill my world caved in. Our neighbors, friends, and many others came to our support, but it wasn't, of course, enough to stave off the desperation of a parent slowly losing a child.

One night there was a knock at our front door. Standing there was the most famous faith healer in our country.

She said, "Hello, I am Kathryn Kuhlman. I don't know why I am here."

I said, "Come in. I will show you why." I had never met her and had not asked her to come to our home. She told me she never made house calls. She had been directed all the way from Long Beach, California to our home in Encino, in the San Fernando Valley, by God. We went into our family room, which we had converted to what we called a

"Life Center" with round-the-clock nurses. We all joined hands and prayed.

Despite our highest hopes, Debbie wasn't miraculously healed. I believed almost to the end that He was telling me that my daughter would be healed while here—but what He had told me was that she would be "all right." That is what I pinned my hopes on, and Kathryn's visit encouraged me on that track.

A friend brought back a vial of water from Lourdes, France, a famous healing site. It was gray and if we had put it under a microscope, it probably would have had every bacillus known to man. It came from the bathing pool of sick people seeking healing; as a sign of faith, the attendants of those who are ill drink some of the water every day. In accordance, we did the same—each drinking half of the vial (I was struggling with cancer myself at the time). Sadly, God did not choose to heal us at that point. As the pain increased for Debbie, I came to the point that I prayed a prayer of release for her. "God, you are the God of justice and mercy. This is not justice and it is not mercy. Heal her now or take her home . . . now." Within ten minutes of that prayer, He took her home. As I look back on these moments I believe God was telling me that Debbie would not be healed on this earth, but rather in heaven. She was all right—more than all right—once home in heaven.

I know she is in radiant health now, because she is in heaven. I know that people asleep to Christ tend to believe that miracles are hogwash. But folks, they are reality. And Debbie's death was a huge turning point in my relationship with God. For years, I could not care whether I lived or died. But slowly, ever so slowly, he brought me back to life—and so much more.

When you read, "I in you, you in Me," there is only one interpretation of His meaning (John 15:5). His love is such that He wants to be a Best Friend of yours. He wants to offer Himself to you, and you to offer yourself to Him. Every person is invited to become best friends with God. That God can be "best" friends with every person remains a mystery—beyond our human understanding or human capability. But it is entirely within the capacity and heart of an infinite, loving God.

Friendship Is Relationship

Friendship involves a mutuality of giving and receiving—it is a relationship. From the beginning, that is what God desired between Himself and His creation. He longed for the fellowship of a creature with the free will to enter into fellowship, or deny it. Jesus taught us that we are His friends, if we do what He commands (John 15:14). In the highest expression of love, He sacrificed Himself for the relationship He wanted with His creation—true friendship (John 15:13). He longed for the intimacy that comes from knowing Him as Father and Creator, even as He knows His children and His creation. Does God desire a relationship with *every* person He has created? Indeed, He does. God desires a relationship with *you*, and He desires that the relationship be that of "intimate friend." In our divine friendship with God, we give ourselves to Him and He gives Himself to us. Nothing can be more precious or profound.

Like a true friend, God does not force the relationship. He invites us, beckons us to desire the relationship, and to enter into it with all that we are and ever hope to be.

Christ says to you, "Give me your heart. I will come and live within you" (see Ephesians 3:17). When that occurs, a relationship is forged that makes failure impossible. You have a relationship with the infinite, all-powerful, and all-knowing God. He never fails! And because He is in you, and your identity is fully in Him, *you* can never fail! Nothing can defeat you—no enemy, not even death.

The apostle Paul said it so well:

Who shall separate us from the love of Christ? Shall tribulation, or distress, or persecution, or famine, or nakedness, or peril, or sword? . . .

But in all these things we overwhelmingly conquer through Him who loved us. For I am convinced that neither death nor life, nor angels, nor principalities, nor powers, nor things present, nor things to come, nor height, nor depth, nor any other created thing, shall be able to separate us from the love of God, which is in Christ Jesus our Lord. (ROMANS 8:35, 37–39 NAST)

Friendship is not rooted in religion, although worship is most definitely involved. Friendship is not bound up in ritual, although traditions certainly develop between friends. Think about your relationships with other men and women. Friendship is communicating, loving, sharing, knowing. It is this kind of relationship that God hungers for from you.

Good attaches itself to good. God is good. The best of you becomes linked to the Best there is, and in the process of the developing friendship, God bestows His character and rewards upon those who seek to know Him intimately. What could possibly be better for you than knowing—really *knowing*—the Light of the World as your Best Friend?

I had a home in Maui for over twenty years. "Aloha," in its broadest and most precise definition, means: "I give all of my love to you." What does it mean to give all your love to God? Are you holding back a little—or a lot—of what you might give Him?

Friendship Involves a Process

No genuine and deep friendship emerges full-blown in the moment two persons are introduced. In truth, nothing happens instantly or "overnight" in the world in which we live. In fact, in order to come up with something happening instantly and overnight, you probably need to go back to Creation! And then, it was God doing the instant creation and implementation. Human beings are incapable of instant creation, instant implementation, or instant processing. We are creatures bound in time, and we develop and grow over time.

My life's work has been focused on developing, testing, and refining effective processes. Deciphering what might be and then turning the "what" into "how" are two inseparable and vitally important steps toward constructing a good strategic plan. Both the creation of the plan and the implementation of the plan involve processes.

To truly understand friendship with God, or with anyone else, a person must catch a glimpse of understanding about *what* a deep and intimate friendship might be, in comparison to the present state of the relationship. A person must then discover or learn *how* to move from what *is* to what *might be.*

Process begins with perspective—with an awareness of what is and what is possible. To be even more accurate, process begins with developing a *right* perspective about what *really* is and what *really* is possible. Reality is only as accurate as one's perspective.

A Spiritual Life That's Real

Has anyone ever told you to "live in the real world?" I've heard that phrase in the business community a great deal in the last forty years, and I may have given it as advice to some who prefer pie-in-the-sky theory to the practicalities of life.

I am primarily interested in knowing more about the "processes" of life—the *real* processes that can be understood in terms of *how* things function. I want to know what works—and works well. I want to know what steps need to be taken, how, and in which order so I might reach specific identifiable and definable goals. I want a real life that functions in a real world with real processes, real how-to's, and real achievable goals.

You probably agree.

Where we might disagree is on this: I want my *spiritual* life to be as real as any other aspect of my life because my spiritual life *is* my life. Boil everything else down to what lasts and what's important and you are going to come up with things that are spiritual. If your spiritual life isn't "real," you're missing a part of your real life—a life that God wants to be as rich and full as possible.

Most people I have met in my life regard spiritual things as mysterious, unknown, vague, "seen through a glass darkly," or in some way, unfathomable. They regard the real world as the world they can see, hear, taste, smell, and touch. To them the spiritual world is otherworldly—it is a dimension that cannot be fully known and therefore isn't as real as the tangible world.

For most people . . .

The *real* world is the tangible, natural world that can be known.

The *mysterious* world is the intangible, spiritual world that cannot be known.

There's only one problem with that.

Jesus said it should be the other way around! He said the *spiritual* world is the real world. It's the world that should become clear to us. It is the world we should know the most about! (see 2 Peter 2:5, 9).

If we are to see things as they *are*, and as they are shaping up to be, we must develop a correct perspective about what is real and what is illusion—not from our earthly perspective, but from God's perspective. As Christians, our anchor in developing God's perspective is the Word of God.

Let's address a little further this issue of illusion and reality.

The older I get, the less I am sure what reality is. Much of what *appears* real is only illusion. We may appear to be solid, but we know from science that we are not. Atomic physics gave way to subatomic physics. We gave names to odd particles—quarks, for example. Strangely enough, quarks kept disappearing. So, scientists came to grasp the concept that everything is energy. Field theory emerged. The natural conclusion was that we are more "space" than "solid." Some things are simply denser than others.

There is a vast difference between illusion and reality in virtually all dimensions of life. Consider the following statements under the caption "Illusion"—things many people spend decades believing to be "real." Bonnie May, my friend and caregiver, remembers a wonderful line in a very old movie: "Illusions are dangerous people: they have no faults." Illusions always appear perfect. On the other hand, there are a number of things that we sometimes come to realize *are* real in spite of decades believing otherwise:

ILLUSION

- "Things are the source of a sense of well-being; the more I can buy, the happier I'll be."

- "I can be whatever I want to become."

- "I don't need God in my life."

- "God isn't real."

- "Satan doesn't exist."

- "Being a believer is all I need to lead a fulfilled life."

REALITY

- "Money can easily rule my life." *Reality!*

- "I can become what God shaped me to become." *Reality!*

- "We are here to glorify God by loving and serving others." *Reality!*

- "God is love and love is our deepest need." *Reality!*

- "This world and all that is in it is from God. He is the Master Designer. We are His vision." *Reality!*

- "Satan is the ruler of this planet." *Reality!*

- "The path of an abundant life—the one-hundredfold life—is one used only by His saints. Surrender is the way to sainthood." *Reality!*

I am firmly convinced that we are called to live in a new reality. When we become friends of God (more on that in chapter 3) we become new, inside and out. We are put into a new dimension of life where suddenly everything is more real than we ever imagined. The old "us" has passed away and truly, *all* things have become new.

I am firmly convinced that God wants to save all of us. He wants every person to live a joyous, fulfilled life—a life at peace with Him, ourselves, and the world at large. A believer's destiny is to find her being in Him. We are here to serve Him. That is what's real. HE is reality.

Truly to "get real" is to know God as our Father. It is to accept His Son, Jesus Christ, as the One who saves us from sin's grip. It is to be filled with God's Holy Spirit and live a new life that He both prescribes and enables us to live.

Beyond the Gospels, the New Testament writers repeatedly proclaim that the real world is the spirit world. Everything in the natural world flows first from the spiritual world. The process begins in the spirit and manifests itself in the natural.

If we want to "get real," we need to "get into the spiritual."

Do you find yourself asking, "Ohhh-kaaay, Tom. How do I do *that*?"

You are not alone! Many believers have told me they have very little understanding about how to "get real" when it comes to the spiritual. For too many years that was certainly true of me. I don't believe, however, that Jesus would have told us to get real about the spiritual if He didn't think we *could*. I don't believe the apostle Paul and other writers of the New Testament would have told us that the spiritual reality was the important reality in which we live and move and have our being if they didn't think it was possible. The truth is, the spiritual life in Christ Jesus *can* be understood and pursued as the greatest reality. We can "get real" about matters of spiritual growth and maturity.

Where Do We Begin?

Have you ever felt that Christianity as practiced by most Christians is long on talk and short on living out a vibrant friendship with God? I have! Much of the talk in our churches focuses on trying to understand a little more about who God the Father is, who Jesus is, and who the Holy Spirit is. Sometimes we don't even deal with that—focusing instead on what a good church does and what a good church member ought to do.

Where we fall woefully short is in gaining perspective on these critical "what is real" issues:

- What are the characteristics of an immature believer in Christ Jesus?

- What are the characteristics of a mature believer in Christ Jesus?

- What are the characteristics of a sold-out Christian?

- What are the characteristics of an abundant life in Christ Jesus?

- What are the characteristics of a person who is experiencing the grace of God?

- What are the characteristics of a person who has been empowered by the Spirit of God?

- What are the characteristics of a Christian who is growing in faith?

If we can't answer these questions that deal with perspective, we don't have much understanding of the overall process of growth and maturity in the Christian life.

Unless we understand the process of spiritual transformation and growth, we can't know where we are in the process! If we can't define a "mature" believer in Christ Jesus, how can we understand how to move from immaturity to maturity? If we don't know the qualities of an abundant life, how can we know if what we are currently doing on a day-to-day basis will produce such a life?

Perspective gives definitions, framework, descriptions, and a clear understanding of what is, what will be if nothing changes, and what *can be* if certain changes are made.

Because very few Christians have a clear perspective on the spiritual life that *can be* theirs in Christ Jesus, they are also woefully short on good "how-to's" when it comes to living the Christian life.

It may be helpful to pause at this point and ask and answer some reflective questions. Keep your answers simple—don't overanalyze! If you don't know the answers, just move on; the purpose of this book is to identify where we are on the walk of faith and how to move on to the next LifeGate. I'm confident that if you don't have any answers for the questions below, you will by the time you finish reading this book.

1. What are the characteristics of a mature believer in Christ?

_____

_____

_____

2. What are the characteristics of an abundant life in Christ Jesus?

_____

_____

_____

3. What are the characteristics of a person who is experiencing the grace of God?

_____

_____

_____

4. What are the characteristics of a Christian who is growing in faith?

_____

_____

_____

Okay, now consider these next questions. Just write a sentence or two—again, I'm aiming to help you figure out where you are now and where you are going next. No one will read it but you.

- How can I be a good Christian?

- How can I develop spiritual maturity?

- How can I grow closer to the Lord?

- How can I know for sure that I am doing the right thing?

- How can I evaluate where I am in my faith walk?

- How will I know I have developed spiritual maturity?

Do you have clear, concise, provable answers?

Or do you just hope that if you continue to do what you've been doing that you will somehow arrive at a place you can't really define?

Here is a helpful acrostic for HOW that my caregiver, Bonnie May, taught me:

H Honesty
O Open-mindedness
W Willingness

"How" requires these three values applied on all fronts.

My conclusion is this: We who make up the body of Christ have very little understanding of the *process* that transforms an unbeliever into a spiritually mature Christian, and unless we understand the process, we aren't going anywhere very effectively, efficiently, or fast. We *must* wake up as Christians and get a clear understanding about where we are going, and how to get there.

That's what this book is all about.

The Process
of Transcending

God's Word outlines for us a transcendence process that covers the "whats" and "hows" of the Christian life. Those who seek God embark on a journey, or a path that takes the person upward and onward spiritually—including onward and upward into eternity. Like all processes, transcendence to living on the Divine level can be segmented into "stages." Although these stages may vary in length of time from person to person, they do not vary in sequence. All people who embark on a spiritual journey go through the same stages in the same sequence, regardless of culture, nationality, race, age, or sex. Between the stages we have what I call "LifeGates." These amount to trigger points—they are events, circumstances, or actions that compel a person to move from one stage to the next. The circumstance or event of a LifeGate is different for each person. The circumstance is initially "external" but quickly becomes "internal."

Why be concerned with these stages and LifeGates? Most of us have an innate but very real need to know where we are spiritually, where we are in the midst of our relationship with God. As with any relationship we wish to grow, we need both validation and challenge. We benefit also by gaining an understanding about where others around us may be in their spiritual walk. Having these insights makes us better evangelists and edifiers. Perhaps most importantly, we each need to be challenged to move to an even higher level in our spiritual life. We need to be encouraged and admonished to grow into the fullness of life that God desires for us to experience and enjoy. We need to know *how* to become even more intimate in our friendship with the Lord.

We also gain insight as we look back to where we have been. The truth is, we all begin at the same place spiritually—we begin "asleep."

Therefore be imitators of God as dear children.
And walk in love, as Christ also has loved us
and given Himself for us, an offering and a
sacrifice to God for a sweet-smelling aroma.

—EPHESIANS 5:1—2

chapter 2

The Stages of Transcendence

The Path of the Christ-Filled Life

I perceive eight stages of transcendence within which are what I term the seven LifeGates. A LifeGate is a supra turning point in your life. Your future will be markedly different than your past. A decision for Christ as your Savior—conversion—is a LifeGate—as is surrender. As this book has been developed around these stages, it is wise to briefly explain each stage of the transformation process:

ASLEEP	A life asleep to our Lord is a counterfeit life, a half life, not the joyous, full life promised by Jesus (John 15:11).
AWAKING FROM SLEEP	LifeGate 1: Man is born with a basic conflict within him. We are born with a free will and must choose between good and evil, love and hatred (Ephesians 1:4).

SEEKING AND FINDING LifeGate 2: The Spirit awakens. Seekers recognize that God is knocking at the door of their heart. It may be through a personal encounter with a believer, a sermon, a gentle nudge that will not go away, prayer, or some other introduction to God's love for us. But a response is required of us. In truth it is God seeking us (Ephesians 5:14).

CONVERTING LifeGate 3: The Spirit converts. We are birthed into the Kingdom and become a new person in Christ. Jesus said that it is essential to enter the Kingdom of God that we are born of water and the Spirit (John 3:5).

YIELDING LifeGate 4: Yielding is present-active tense. We choose to claim the fullness of a life in Christ. God wants us to not only accept Jesus as Savior (Conversion) but to yield to Him as Lord. The fullness of a life in Christ requires that moment by moment, step by step, day by day, we are guided by our Lord, and hear the ongoing voice of the Holy Spirit, deep within our spirit (2 Chronicles 30:8).

SURRENDERING LifeGate 5: In Yielding we accept Jesus as our Lord; in Surrendering we deny self and choose to live the life He pours into and through us. He takes full hold of us. Unless we surrender none of us can do the higher works God has ordained for us (2 Chronicles 30:8, Romans 6:13).

ANOINTING

LifeGate 6: It is through the LifeGate of Anointing that the Holy Spirit unleashes a person's full potential for service. The Holy Spirit calls-"installs" a person as a God-"appointed" servant. We cannot anoint ourselves (Luke 4:18).

SANCTIFIED SERVING

LifeGate 7: Jesus is our role model when it comes to service. His earthly life is our example. We are heirs of God and joint heirs with Him and are free to accept our birthright. "Follow Me" or not. It's our choice; it is not a burden. It is our privilege. It is the source of fulfillment, purpose, a meaningful life and exhilarating joy. God's plan is for His children to be witnesses of His grace, ministers of His mercy and compassion (Romans 6:19).

To master our life as a Christian we must live according to God's will and His rules (2 Timothy 2:5).

In the mid-1970s I was living in Northridge, California, and significantly remodeled our home. I bought two custom oak doors for the front entrance and asked my carpenter to install them. He said that he would not do it. "They require a master, Tom."

"How do I get a master?"

"The door company will have two or three."

I purchased these doors from the largest door manufacturer in Southern California. I called them: "Do you have master door hangers?"

"We have three," was their answer.

I asked, "Whom do I wait for longest?"

They gave me his name and I asked for his phone number. I would have to wait several weeks, and I did so gladly. My carpenter asked me if he could come over and watch the master install my beautiful doors.

I was working at the dining room table, which was within feet of where the doors were being installed. My carpenter asked the door installer: "How did you become a master?"

He replied, "Son, I studied every step of the process. Next, I learned how to do it as well as it could possibly be done. Third, I then learned how to do it as rapidly as it could be done. And those, my boy, are the keys to making money hanging custom doors."

I have always marveled at his wisdom. In fact, these are the keys to mastering everything: painting, sculpting, architecture . . . and becoming an Everyday Saint*:

1. Know every step.

2. Do each step of the process as well as it can be done.

3. Do each step as rapidly as it can possibly be done.

By "rapidly," I do not mean rush it. Think *no mistakes*. With every step, just try to get it right the first time. In China, students learn to make an ideograph that conveys all the intelligence and emotion to be conveyed in a single stroke. They cannot go back and fudge it here and there to make it right. That's what I'm getting at—we need to become so adept and aware of what we're doing that we model excellence, even in our developing spirituality.

---

* I don't think the term Everyday Saint originated with me; I would credit the source if I could remember it.

A tremendous void in the Church is the near absence of pastoral training in human behavior. Very few Christians come to the absolute surrender that Andrew Murray wrote about more eloquently than any other pastor: "The soul utterly given up to God will receive in its emptying the fullness of the Holy Spirit." We must be empty vessels if we wish for God to fill us with more of Him.

Make the teachings of Jesus who you are; so internalized that you do not have to stop and think about the correct response in a given situation.

Through God's Word we can know all of Jesus' teachings. In John 15:15 (NASB) Jesus says: "I have called you friends, for all things that I have heard from my Father I have made known to you."

The spiritual transcendence process is essentially one from sinner to fully surrendered, anointed-for-sanctified-service Everyday Saint. I think of this process as an ongoing path for the believer, one each of us is walking. There is no finish line on this earth, and, I suspect, not in heaven either. The path is also one of an upward progression. When we transcend we go beyond our best, we surpass, rise above. We also transform, change our nature as part of the transcendence process. The Lord does not desire to "fix" you. He creates. He is the Creator and He desires to create a new life within you.

As a believer, you are a pilgrim. Dictionary.com defines "pilgrim" not as those early New Worlders who settled America, but rather as "a person who journeys, esp. a long distance, to some sacred place as an act of religious devotion." This world is not your destination. Our "journey to a sacred place" is actually our sojourn here on Earth, en route to heaven. You might be wise to pause and ask yourself, "Where am I in my pilgrimage?" "Which descriptions best apply to me?" "Which descriptions best outline the future I want?" "Is my ultimate destination heaven?" "Do I know I'll reach my destination?"

I encourage you to pause for reflection. Ask the Holy Spirit to reveal to you what He desires for you. Ask Him to show you His path for your becoming the person with whom our Heavenly Father wants to spend eternity. Ask Him to reveal what He desires to cleanse, purify, and transform within you.

Evaluate as well your own readiness to take the next step in your spiritual life. Thomas Merton wrote: "Time is given to us not to keep a faith we once had but to acquire a faith we need now." The journey never ends this side of heaven, friends. There's always a new step we can take, a new discovery we can make about the spiritual life, and life in relationship with God.

Are *you* ready to let God remake the substance of your life: all things new, inside and out?

His love is in a tender glance, and in the
golden moments of dawn;
His Love is in softly spoken words of prayer,
and in the streams of sun dappling the silent forest floor.
His Love is in the touch of a hand, which, without words, says,
"I care," and in the glorious promise of a rainbow,
Which gives us hope. His Love is in an unexpected kindness,
and in the shining sea, which cries, "See me, enjoy me!"
His Love is in the air; it's everywhere . . . eternity visiting earth,
a glimpse of heaven within time; life itself . . .
For to love is to live and be loved.
Seize it, give it to all, live it, and experience God.
Life will never be the same again, for with each new day,
You will become more like Him.

ETERNITY

LifeGate 7: Sanctified Service

LifeGate 6: Anointing

LifeGate 5: Surrendering

LifeGate 4: Yielding

LifeGate 3: Converting

LifeGate 2: Seeking

LifeGate 1: Awakening

Asleep

Seven LifeGates:
The stairway to the transcendent life in the here and now.

chapter 3

Awakening from Sleep

LifeGate 1

A re you *awake and ready* to receive the Lord's forgiveness and then to forgive yourself for whatever it is you regret? Are you ready to forget the sins and sorrows of the past and move forward?

The Lord Jesus is waiting for you. He desires to forgive you and help you move beyond your past. He is ready to accomplish something totally new in you and through you.

Are you *awake and ready* to let go and let God guide your life? Are you ready to let go of everything else and cooperate fully with Him?

God is calling you to be His friend and His partner in accomplishing His plans and purposes for you and others around you.

Are you *awake and ready* to submit to the Lord's will, to complete union with God "face-to-face?" Are you ready to encounter the absolute fullness of truth, life, and good?

In receiving *truth*, you must be willing to open your heart and mind to understanding, wisdom, and the happiness that comes with not only knowing but living out the Truth of God—His Word. As we learn more from the scriptures, we find that His ways and judgments are altogether true and righteous, faithful, loving, kind, good, and just. And we begin to strive to be and do the same as our Father.

In receiving *life*, you must be willing to receive the fullness of life that can be experienced only through Christ Jesus as the Holy Spirit leads and guides you day by day.

In receiving *good*, you must be willing to move into union with God. Jesus said, "No one is good but God alone" (Mark 10:17–18 NASB). He is the One who makes us good by His presence, and His presence alone. In the absolute sense, "Lord" is a term reserved for God alone. Jesus was responding here, to someone who did not recognize His divinity, that He was one with the Lord, ready to do His bidding.

Are you *awake and ready* to love the cross and to pick it up as Christ did—to live a life of obedience focused on those things that have even a seed of eternal benefit within them? Taking up His cross means that you are willing to live the holy life as one of God's Everyday Saints.

If your answers to these questions above is an unqualified "Yes," then mark the moment. God is moving in you, birthing the impossible.

There Must Be Something More

Man is born with an intuitive awareness that he is not alone, and that some type of supreme being exists.

The noted anthropologist Margaret Mead was one of the first people to document the cultures of the South Seas. She wrote that she found among all of the primitive peoples of the South Pacific an innate sense of a higher authority. Other anthropologists have confirmed her conclusion in their work among primitive peoples in other parts of the world. In countless cases, this awareness lies dormant within the individual. People are "asleep," so to speak, when it comes to an awareness of the higher reality of their own spirituality.

In this sleeping phase, man is unconsciously incompetent. He doesn't know what he doesn't know. He has an attitude that he is self-sufficient and can be a "good person" on his own efforts. He trusts in himself. The moment we awake we are consciously incompetent.

Man trusts in himself in part because he is a creature of free will, which means that he is capable of creating and innovating within the greater laws of God's creation. Man can make choices and decisions, and act on them, bearing the consequences of those choices and decisions with an ongoing exertion of his will to bring about change in his world. Our life is shaped and determined by the choices we make.

It was a cold winter night in my Big Bear, California home, some 7,400 feet in the mountains. I bundled up in my overcoat and went outside to talk with God. I asked Him why, if I have a free will, He would have His way in the end.

He explained: "Let's say you are a fish and I am a fisherman. I get you hooked. You can fight me but I am going to have my way with you. I will bring you in because I have special work for you to do." The exercise of free will—and the creative result of using that will—gives man a tremendous feeling of personal power and authority. Even so, every person inevitably runs into limitations. There is an end to what man can choose for himself. As the old saying goes, my freedom ends at your nose. As much as we have a will to choose and decide, we are faced with compromise . . . continually.

In addition, we quickly discover that although we have a free will to choose and decide, we do *not* have a free will when it comes to determining the inevitable consequences of our choices and decisions. Those are fixed! We can choose to jump off a cliff after making a decision that we *will* fly . . . only to discover that there is a greater fixed law of consequences awaiting us in the form of a "law of gravity" that pulls us to the ravine below. I think of the man who jumped off a hundred-story building. As he sailed down and passed the eightieth floor he was heard to say: "so far, so good." In like manner, we can choose to violate all sorts of moral and ethical rules that have fixed consequences. We can act, but we cannot alter or avoid the consequences of our actions.

Are we doomed to failure, then? Not at all.

We do not *need* to make choices that have negative consequences. We *can* choose good.

Some people believe that we have a fixed nature from birth—that we are intrinsically evil or divine. I believe we are neither devils nor angels. Rather, we are human beings with a divine will to *choose* evil or good.

God, of course, is the One who defines evil and good. What God declares as good . . . is good! What God states is evil . . . is evil! We are not given the opportunity, responsibility, privilege, or burden of defining what is right and wrong. We are only given the opportunity to *choose* what we will say, do, think, and believe against a backdrop of good and evil.

From the beginning, man has had difficulty in being obedient to the will of God. Disobedience began in the Garden of Eden. Satan whispered, Eve encouraged, and Adam disobeyed. The discord resulting from disobedience has come down through the ages.

We are at odds with ourselves from birth. We want what we should not want. We do not do what we know we should do. We do not want what is good for us; we choose what is bad for us—willfully in many cases, and unwittingly in other cases. We cannot stop this within ourselves by ourselves. Neither can we stop it between ourselves and other people by ourselves. Only Christ can put a stop to this bondage and give us a *desire* to choose what God says is good. Only Christ can free us from the propensity to choose evil. Peace within, and peace between people, comes only through Christ.

As I write, we are again at war—this time a war against "terrorism." We are dealing with evil flowing from people who are willfully choosing what is *evil* according to God's definitions (even though they may be so blinded in their hatred that they perceive evil to be good). Hear the words of Jesus: "A good person produces good deeds from a good heart, and an evil person produces evil deeds from an evil heart. Whatever is in your heart determines what you say" (Luke 6:45 NLT). Jesus might have added, "And determines what you think and do."

Throughout Scripture—and intuitively among even the most primitive peoples of the earth—hatred is perceived as evil. The slaughter of innocents—the demise of innocence—is perceived as evil. The shackling of the human spirit is perceived as evil. And in sharp contrast, love is perceived as good, the building up of human life and all that is pure and lovely, and the promotion of freedom are perceived as good. All tyrants hate freedom, abhor the concept of triumphant love, and refuse to acknowledge the value of innocence. This has been true throughout history and always will be. In dealing with terrorism, we are dealing with evil choices made by human will.

Jesus stated very clearly during His earthly ministry that He came to set us free. He said, "If you abide in My word, you are My disciples indeed. And you shall know the truth, and the truth shall make you free" (John 8:31–32 NKJV).

The religious leaders of Jesus' day, the Pharisees, were amazed at Jesus' teaching. They responded, "We are Abraham's descendants and have never been in bondage to anyone. How can you say, "You will be made free?" Now, in reality, they had known plenty of bondage through the centuries—at the hands of Egyptians, Assyrians, Babylonians, and at the time they spoke, the Romans. They were in total denial of that truth when they replied to Jesus as they did. They could not discern truth because they did not choose to acknowledge Him as the Source of truth.

Jesus did not challenge the Pharisees. Rather, He simply replied, "Truly, truly I say to you, Everyone who commits sin is the slave of sin. And the slave does not remain in the house forever; the son does remain forever. If therefore the Son shall make you free, you shall be free indeed" (John 8:34–36 NAST). Because the Pharisees did not *believe*, they heard the Word but could not understand it. They were not free, and did not know that they were not free. In reality, they were their own jailers as a result of their disbelief.

Many people today are asleep . . . and enslaved in their thinking . . . for the very same reason. Some do not know they are asleep. Still others hear the call to awake but they choose not to respond.

What we human beings cannot choose, however, is to feel free from guilt or free from the inner conflict that arises when we willfully choose not to be awakened from our sleep.

Willingly Asleep

There are those who spend years feeling fine about not being awakened. I'll give you a good example. Monica prayed for her son for twenty years. She asked God if she could stop praying for him. God told her to continue praying. Her son would say: "I want to be good, but later." He was a notorious womanizer.

Monica continued in prayer for her boy. He became St. Augustine (of the Confessions). They both became saints of the Catholic Church.

The conflict in man is deep-seated. It springs from our unwillingness to accept our role in the grand order of His plan.

Satan whispers, "You can be a god. You can be the master of your own fate. Take charge." What a lie that is! We cannot be whatever we want. Millions of people pursue that lie only to discover—at some point in their life, early or late—that it is, indeed, a lie. As I say, if a person doesn't have the natural talent or gift to be a musician, that person can become at best a proficient "hack." If a person isn't *allowed* to form relationships and to enter situations conducive to personal goals, that person is not likely to reach his goals. Unless a person has the *wisdom* to make certain choices and decisions, a person can be in the right place with the right gifts and still not realize the fullness of her own potential. Wisdom is *imparted* to a person by the Spirit of God. Wisdom is not self-manufactured no matter how much information gathering a person may do. A human being simply cannot manufacture or engineer his own life to reach the pinnacle of fame, wealth, power, or even health that he might desire. Other factors, and primarily the awesome God factor, are always involved.

Yet, man tries. He strives. He kicks against the inevitable truth that no man can ever *be* God. No man can ever *be* the master of his own fate. No man has the power, ability, capacity, intelligence, or insight to take charge of all that needs to be controlled, acquired, or excised.

Deep within, every person knows that he cannot be the absolute master of his own destiny. He cannot give himself eternal life, nor can he earn it. He knows that there is very little that he can control—his primary ability is to adapt, control what he can control. There is no amount of self-motivation of self-improvement—no amount of reason or creative imagination—that can produce in any person divine authority.

Fools say, "I'll change the wind."

Realists say, "I'll adjust the sails."

H. G. Wells once observed, "Religion is the first thing and the last thing, and until a man has found God, he begins at no beginning and works to no end." Life falls into place only through Him.

In the end, our revolt against the Infinite God is a revolt against our own nature. We remain in a fundamental conflict with ourselves—we strive to be what we cannot be, and in so doing, we fail to become what we were designed to become.

Harmony in the universe would be impossible if God were to break His own rules. We create discord and cause our own suffering (as we have since the Garden of Eden) by breaking His rules. We are collectively running our lives contrary to God's will and contrary to His governing principles in the universe.

We can only save our lives by losing them to God. We can only enter into close relationship with God the Father—and truly become best friends with Him—through obedience to His rules. His rules govern our relationships, feelings, choices, decisions, including our relationship and feelings and choices related to Him! What we choose to do with regard to His rules shapes our future. We become what we think and feel. We make choices and decisions in light of what we think and feel. We behave either as obedient and surrendered children, or as rebellious and wayward children.

The end of self-centeredness is destruction.

The end of God-centeredness is life, now and forever.

The Life Gate of "Awakening"

For a person to move from the first stage of Sleeping to the next stage in the transcendence process, a person must have an awakening of some type. Something happens to "quicken" spiritual awareness. The person comes alive to the possibility that there is more to his earthly existence than the physical, natural, or material. He becomes aware of his need for God. He experiences a longing to know his Creator.

I went to China for President Reagan in 1982 as part of a small delegation to help open up China and develop their economy. They specifically asked for a Chinese individual, Wun Chiou, to come as part of the delegation. Wun was living in San Jose, California, and came from a very distinguished family. I was told by the Chinese officials we met with that there is an entire mountain range in China named for his family.

We had made arrangements with the American consul in Shanghai to be in prayer for our mission at noon on Friday, the last day of our week in China. He ushered our four-person delegation—one of our group being Dr. Vernon Grose—into a beautiful setting aglow with light. Three of us knelt at chairs; Wun stood in a corner, respectfully, hands clasped, head down. At that exact time, Vernon's pastor, Jack Hayford, had assembled some eight hundred people holding candles at his Church On The Way in Southern California.

Precisely one year later to the day and hour, Wun Chiou called me from his home. "Where were we a year ago, Tom?"

I thought for a moment and said, "We were in Shanghai."

Next, he asked, "What was happening at this exact time?"

"Three of us were kneeling in prayer."

"What was I doing?" he asked.

"You were standing in a corner, respectfully, with your hands folded and head down."

He said, "I waited a year to tell you that was the exact moment of my conversion. I have been active in the church ever since. My wife's mother, a former missionary, never stopped praying for me."

I told Wun that God had much more in mind than our helping to open up China. In that moment, he experienced the quickening of the heart needed to finally awake.

The apostle Paul briefly addressed this LifeGate in his opening statements to the church in Rome:

> *What may be known of God is manifest in them . . . for since the creation of the world His invisible attributes are clearly seen, being understood by the things that are made, even His eternal power and Godhead, so that they are without excuse.*
>
> (ROMANS 1:19–20 NKJV)

In other words, Paul is stating that all of the creation has the capacity to serve as a trigger point for Awaking. God uses His creation to speak to those who are ungodly and unrighteous. At some point, God reaches out to a person in a way that causes that person to recognize that God exists. His voice is stronger than that of the enemy. His whisper to us is truth: "Choose Christ. Choose Him as Savior. Surrender to Him as Lord." This voice of the Spirit whispers the only remedy for our inner turmoil: *Accept the unconditional love of God and totally yield to Him—in complete submission, you will find complete freedom to become all that He has created you to be.*

The Holy Spirit speaks to us deep within our hearts, telling us that we are all God's children. He reveals to us that we have been gifted by God, with both natural and spiritual gifts. As a teenager I would stand in front of a mirror and direct Glen Miller's band on the radio. This was an early indication of a natural gift. Later I learned to play the trumpet and carried it with me while in the service. I would often play at church services while in the military.

Writing and teaching are other gifts God has given me. The Life-Planning Process I developed, and the resulting book, *Living the Life You Were Meant to Live*, utilize both of those gifts. I would not have the boldness to speak into someone else's life as I do through LifePlanning unless I knew that the Spirit was guiding the entire process. Through thirty years of utilizing the principles of LifePlanning and mentoring others, I've enjoyed amazing experiences and relationships—and one of the most memorable was with Steve Craver (who gave me permission to share his story).

Steve's Plan called for complete uprooting of his life. He was living in Southern California and attending Saddleback Valley Community Church when he came to me for a Plan. The Plan called for him to: (1) move to the heart of the Bible Belt; (2) select a church where he could make a strong contribution and (3) let the church's location determine where he and his family would live; (4) he would purchase a property large enough for other members of his family to have homes and for clients to stay at his home and hold meetings there; and (5) he would continue doing the same work as in California.

We went to dinner on the last night, after finishing the Plan. Steve told me that he needed confirmation. "What will my wife say? This is so radical a move, my world is being turned upside down." I asked him to pray for confirmation that night and told him I would do the same.

About 1:30 a.m. I heard a loud alarm go off. Having been in the military, I recognized the "AaaWhoop, AaaWhoop" as a call to general quarters, battle stations! I awoke and said to my wife, who remained asleep, "Where did you ever get such an alarm? Shut it off!" She never heard the alarm. It stopped in a few seconds and I went back to sleep.

In the morning Steve asked me if we could walk our grounds, see the gardens. Everywhere I have lived I have developed beautiful gardens. After we toured the yard we stood out front, on the driveway. There was a pause in our conversation. I asked, "Did you hear the alarm?"

Steve smiled and said, "Did I hear it? It was in my room. I awoke, got up, put my palm on the bedroom door to see if it was hot. It wasn't, so I went upstairs looking for a fire. There wasn't any. I went back to my bedroom and knelt to pray. God interrupted my prayer and said, Steve, you hear the waterfall just outside your window. I am in that water. There is a redwood tree in the corner of the garden. I am in its bark. I am in the blood coursing through your veins. And, I am in your Plan. Now, just do it!"

Steve went home. His wife accepted the Plan. They moved near Nashville, in the heart of the Bible Belt. The location was determined by the church God led him to. He has about 1,700 square feet of meeting space and he has all the business he can possibly handle. God is in the plan, indeed!

———————

God imparts to us a peace of soul that comes as we lay down our will and request the impartation of His will. The Holy Spirit is the author of our reconciliation with the Father—a reconciliation that sets us on a path toward true wholeness and holiness. Incidentally, the Catholic Church no longer speaks of confession. It is now reconciliation.

The person who chooses to trust in his own abilities cannot rest in the infinite trustworthiness of God.

The person who trusts in his own goodness cannot experience the true and lasting goodness of the Spirit flowing deep within himself, and then *through* his gifts and skills to others in need.

It simply is not possible to serve self and God at the same time.

God does not yield to us. We yield to Him.

Most of us are not, and never will be, in a position to end the wars between other people, much less cultures, religions, or nations in conflict. We can, however, make the choice to end the conflict within ourselves. We can know Christ's peace. As Romans tells us, For the mind set on the flesh is death, but the mind set on the Spirit is life and peace because the mind set on the flesh is hostile toward God; for it does not subject itself to the law of God, for it is not even able to do so; and those who are in the flesh cannot please God (Rom. 8:6–8 NAST).

True harmony, tranquility, and fullness of life are possible only through Him. The moment we *awaken* to that truth, we enter a new phase in our spiritual transformation. We become seekers.

ETERNITY

LifeGate 7: Sanctified Service

LifeGate 6: Anointing

LifeGate 5: Surrendering

LifeGate 4: Yielding

LifeGate 3: Converting

LifeGate 2: Seeking

LifeGate 1: Awakening

ASLEEP

Seven LifeGates:
The stairway to the transcendent life in the here and now.

chapter 4

Seeking . . . and Finding
LifeGate 2

Y ou *may have seen this* well-known painting: A person is
knocking on a door. It has no handle to open it from the outside.
Jesus is on the other side awaiting the knock of a seeker. The handle
to open the door is on the inside. He will open the door.

It is not the person who "finds God." Rather, it is God who reaches
out to embrace the awakened seeker in a way that the seeker recognizes it is God who is knocking at the door and the seeker must respond. The door is not some mystical place; the door can be found
where we find Love, embodied. As humans we need love in our lives.
God is love. We need love.

Love is the supreme characteristic of God. "God is Love" (1 John
4:8). To know God we must live in love. He loved us first. If I live a
love-filled life, I am God-filled, the door is continually open. But too
many of us live with the door barely open. "Sipping Christianity"
leads to a form of immunity to Christianity, as Søren Kierkegaard
pointed out. This is why he said, "It is easier to become a Christian
when I am not one than to become a Christian when I am one." Some
of us believe the cracked door is enough, and so we remain partially

asleep, rather than fully engaged in the search—longing for total immersion in our Creator.

God hungers for a self-sacrificing love from every believer. God's "reaching out" is never thwarted by fears we face in considering self-sacrifice; He continues to woo, continues to extend His mercy and love, and continues to call to the deepest core of a person's being. And He calls us to embody his love. God's command: "Thou shalt love thy neighbor as thyself" is an absolute. There are no options in it. Mother Teresa said: "Only God can do great things. But we can do small things with Great love."

In the Seeking stage, the person sins, but he knows he has sinned against himself and his fellow man. He feels guilt, perhaps shame. The knowledge that he has sinned does not bring with it a genuine release from the resulting guilt or shame—rather, the greater the knowledge of sin, the greater the feeling of guilt or shame. The person continues to have an intuitive sense that a higher authority or power exists, and with this sense, there comes a desire to connect with that higher authority or power in some way—often with the hope that the higher power will alleviate his feelings of guilt and shame.

The longer the person remains in the Seeking stage, the more the person develops a receptivity toward Christ and His love, forgiveness, and presence.

Don't Be Discouraged!

If you are willing and eager to move forward in your spiritual transformation but do not see any evidence of forward motion, don't be discouraged. No person I have ever met is fully *satisfied* with the life he or she is presently living. We are all sinners. We each are at different stages in our spiritual growth and transformation. God said, "Let us make man in our image" (Genesis 1:26). Humanity had a moral and natural likeness to God. After the Fall, we lost the moral likeness but retained the natural likeness (the predisposition to love, other emotional qualities, and intellect).

The good news is that God does not desire for us to remain where we are. He desires for us to move forward. He *will* act toward that end, if we are willing to trust Him.

Sometimes the process of growth and transcendence seems painfully slow. Don't become dismayed or allow yourself to slip into a defeated attitude. The Lord will not leave you where you are if you truly desire to yield everything to Him. Trust the Spirit of God to help you to deal with various issues you may need to address in your life, and to change you to His ways, in His timing, by His methods, and always for His purposes.

The LifeGate of Conversion

At the end of the Seeking stage is the LifeGate of Conversion.

A person's decision to move from the Seeking stage through the LifeGate of Conversion is not entirely a matter of human will.

Through the years I have been a great admirer of the work of Abraham Maslow, who is perhaps best known for his "Hierarchy of Human Needs." Maslow's overall premise was this: A person moves from meeting physiological needs to seeking self-actualization (the fulfillment of psychological desires), upward through a series of stages in pyramid fashion. Most people in the world live at the stage of seeking to meet their basic needs for food, shelter, and water. Very few of the world's citizens have their external physical and social needs met to the point that they can seek "internal" satisfaction.

Maslow's hierarchy of human need does not address spiritual issues, but his concepts are applicable to a discussion of spiritual transcendence. Maslow stated that a person cannot *will* himself beyond the meeting of physiological needs—in many cases, others must help. In like manner, a person cannot convert himself. The Holy Spirit is the outside agent of Conversion, wooing the person to Christ and convicting the person of sin.

Jesus said this about the Father wooing us to Christ by means of the Spirit working in our hearts and minds, "No one can come to Me unless the Father who sent Me draws him" (John 6:44 NASB).

Jesus spoke of this on the last night before His crucifixion when He said to His chosen apostles: "I will send Him [the Holy Spirit] to you. And when He has come, he will convict the world of sin, and of righteousness, and of judgment; of sin, because they do not believe in Me; of righteousness, because I go to My Father and you see Me no more; of judgment, because the ruler of this world has been judged" (John 16:7–11 NKJV).

The Holy Spirit brings about a threefold conviction:

- First, an acute awareness of sinfulness that can only be alleviated by faith in Christ Jesus;

- Second, an awareness that one must follow Christ in order to be in right standing with the Father; and

- Third, that there are eternal ramifications of "judgment" related to receiving Jesus as Savior—either a destructive "condemnation for not receiving Christ" or an "eternal reward" for receiving Him.

Jesus is also quoted by John as saying about Himself: "God did not send His Son into the world to condemn the world, but that the world through Him might be saved. He who believes in Him is not condemned; but he who does not believe is condemned already, because he has not believed in the name of the only begotten Son of God. And this is the condemnation, that the light has come into the world, and men loved darkness rather than light, because their deeds were evil" (John 3:17–19 NKJV).

In addition, the New Testament teaches that the "preaching of the Word"—an expression about the Gospel or the "Good News" of Christ Jesus is also a requisite for a person to move from Seeking to Salvation through the LifeGate of Conversion. Paul wrote to the Romans, "How then shall they call on Him in whom they have not believed?

And how shall they believe in Him of whom they have not heard? And how shall they hear without a preacher? . . . Faith comes by hearing and hearing by the word of God" (Romans 10:14, 17 NKJV).

Hearing the Good News

The "hearing" of good news that compels a person through a LifeGate of Conversion does not necessarily mean the hearing of a sermon from a pulpit. Sometimes the message is conveyed far from a church sanctuary, and many times the message is conveyed by a person who is what I call an Everyday Saint.

An Everyday Saint is often a layperson who nonetheless has come to know Christ in a profound way and who, in innocence and purity of heart, conveys the love of God to others in a way that is both winsome and convicting. The New Testament writers teach that a "saint" is any person who believes in Jesus Christ as his or her Savior and seeks to emulate His life on this earth. Everyday Saints include all those who have freely received the forgiveness offered to them by God the Father through Jesus Christ, and in turn are freely forgiving others around them as Jesus taught (see Luke 6:36–37).

My little girl, Debbie, was just such a saint.

At the age of eleven, Debbie was diagnosed with cancer of the spine. That was in the 1960s, long before the more effective treatments of today were discovered. Her health declined quickly and with an unrelenting increase in pain and suffering.

Debbie spent the last few weeks of her life in a small hospital-style room we created in our home. We hired round-the-clock nurses to be at her side. With great care they administered oxygen and pain medications. Everything we knew to do to fight back death and ease my little girl's agony was done.

During those final weeks, Debbie made a concerted effort to apologize to every person who came to her bedside. She apologized for virtually everything she thought she *might* have done to hurt or disappoint them. She sought forgiveness not only from God but from others. Invariably, of course, those who came to her bedside not only extended forgiveness to Debbie—although virtually nobody felt that she had done anything for which apology was warranted—and they in turn sought and received her forgiveness.

In the end, Debbie was not healed . . . physically. But in the process of asking for forgiveness and, in return, receiving it, she truly was made "whole." Even as her physical health declined, God forged her spiritual well-being into something more.

I do not believe for a second that God caused Debbie's disease or her death. I do believe that God can use any situation, even one as terrible as Debbie's, for the furtherance of His plan. Debbie became a saint at a very early age. She lives in the near presence of the Savior. And out of her illness and death, our family life was transformed into one that reflected God's generous love and care.

- I received Christ as my Savior.

- While most marriages end in divorce when their child dies (about 80 percent), Ginny and I pulled together, becoming a stronger witness of His love.

- Our son, Tom, became a pastor.

It was out of my experience of watching our little girl suffer and die that I came to a new understanding about the plan God has for each of us. It is a plan for eternal good—and while we are here on earth, it is a plan for our inner peace, true prosperity, and above all, our spiritual transcendence, gained by surrendering more and more to Him.

Debbie accomplished a great deal for the Kingdom, in a short period of time, by the way in which she chose to seek forgiveness and receive it!

The Hope of Eternal Life

The "Good News" of Jesus Christ is always linked in some way with a hope that involves eternity. The word *"hope"* as used in our Bible comes from the Greek language and means "confident expectation." I have found seventy-two references to "hope" in the Bible. They are fairly evenly split between the Old and New Testaments. Jesus extended to us the promise that those who believe in Him would become the recipients of everlasting life and a heavenly home (see John 3:16). I do not believe it was in any way a marginal side note that it took Debbie's *death* to trigger in me a desire to know that God held out the hope of eternal *life* for me. To be with Debbie again after she died meant being with her in eternity, in the fullness of life everlasting. The Spirit used Debbie's death to bring me to and through the Conversion LifeGate. The experience of longing to see her again brought me back to caring about life.

Losing one of your children is worse than the worst thing you can imagine, unless that is the thing you have imagined. If you have experienced this you know what I mean. Ginny and I were graced with four wonderful children. Three of our children have now passed on: Debbie at age twelve; Tom Jr., our pastor son, at age thirty-seven, killed in a float plane crash in Alaska; Jimmy, hit by a car and killed at age fifty-nine, as he got out of his car to do the Lord's work. And, as you learned at the opening of this book, Ginny is now in heaven.

God's outstretched arms to us are arms that extend from heaven to earth—they reach out to embrace us and pull us closer and closer to His bosom in heaven. The security of His embrace is the security of knowing that we will never be loosed from His embrace. He holds us now. He holds us forever. He holds my loved ones who've passed on before me.

Some time ago I talked to a shopowner in my town. She stated, "I cannot accept the fact that I must die. It seems wrong. I'm having a great time here and I know nothing of any possible other place." I explained that the only way to get out of this world "alive" is to be a believer in Christ Jesus, that the only way to live fully alive in this life is to be a God-filled person. This woman hoped that through self-sufficiency, she could somehow determine her own fate. She wanted to be her own "all in all."

The truth is, she will die. We all will die.

The truth is, we cannot be totally self-sufficient. We all need other people in our lives. We need God.

The truth is, we cannot determine every detail of our own future. We are all subject to trends, influences, the choices and decisions of others around us, and ultimately, the plans and purposes of God.

God said of Himself, "I AM." He is the One who is infinite and self-sufficient unto Himself. When we try to become our own "I am," we enter a state of revolt against the true I AM.

The Hope of Forgiveness

The "Good News" of Jesus Christ is always a message of forgiveness freely received and freely granted. The Good News is also always a message that usually comes to us at a point where we are feeling our greatest need for forgiveness. The "Good News" is often not heard by us until we hit some sort of bottom in our life, which may be a point of failure, a point of great pain, a point of tremendous need or, as in my case, a point of suffering and insufferable grief.

As ecstatic as I had been at the birth of Debbie, I was just that devastated at her death. I hit bottom. I attempted to drown my sorrow and grief in alcohol. It was not a conscious decision, of course, but neither was it an excuse. It was also something that I realized then and now as a failed method. Eventually I was drinking half to three-fourths of a bottle of whiskey a night. But the alcohol never fully numbed my intense pain and grief.

I truly believe that I would not have lived very many years longer had I not made a change in my behavior. There's a Chinese saying, "Man takes a drink. The drink takes a drink. Drink takes the man." When "the drink takes a drink," the drinking is symptomatic. A person drinks out of habit, not desire. The addiction has not fully taken hold at this point, but a person is on the verge of being addicted to alcohol. That's the point at which I found myself.

I finally reached the point one night when I threw my hands in the air and said, "God, take over. I can't handle this." I was instantly cured of my reliance on alcohol. I have never been drunk since that moment over forty years ago. I have no need to turn to alcohol for relief of any inner pain, sorrow, or trouble I experience. I relied instead on the Lord and continue to rely on Him.

I began to seek the Lord to help me with other issues. More specifically, I began to seek the Lord to help me find peace from the grief. When I turned my life over to God, I received that peace. That was my point of conversion, of accepting Jesus as my Savior. It was a significant turning point in my life.

Now, should you wonder about my spiritual life prior to that point of conversion, let me assure you that I had been a churchgoer for years. When I was twelve years old, I presented myself for baptism and membership at the altar of the Methodist church in my local community. Ours was not a churchgoing family. I had good parents, but they did not attend church at any point during my childhood. Why did I take this step on my own at the age of twelve? I believe it was a God-driven experience. I took this initiative without any encouragement or support from family or friends. I got up one Sunday morning and went to church on my own and went to the altar at the appropriate time in the service, was baptized, and joined the church. I began to attend regularly from that point. I was a churchgoer but not converted to Christ. Church attendance and conversion are not synonymous—not even close. Conversion was yet ahead.

Note very closely what Jesus said: "For God so loved the world that He gave His only begotten Son, that whoever *believes* in Him should not perish but have eternal life" (John 3:16 NKJV).

Volumes could be written on the concept that Jesus was the one definitive and complete substitutionary sacrifice for the sins of mankind. I'll summarize here:

- A sacrifice was required to restore what had been "lost" by man's willful sin in the Garden of Eden. God established the concept of sacrifice as a means of restoration between man and God. It was God who killed the first animals to clothe Adam and Eve. In so doing, God made it clear that a blood sacrifice was required to always remind man that God alone was the giver of life (blood being the foremost symbol of life), and therefore, God had the authority to require obedience from man.

- Only the blood sacrifice of an animal "without blemish" was acceptable to God. It is this principle that was at the heart of all the Jewish sacrifices detailed in the Old Testament.

- Jesus became the ultimate sacrificial "Lamb of God." He was God's only begotten Son, miraculously conceived and given to the world for precisely this purpose of sacrifice. Jesus was fully God and fully man—God in human flesh. He did not sin. His death by crucifixion on the cross was the definitive, "final" blood sacrifice required. His crucifixion came during the Passover Feast of the Jews at the precise moment that the high priest in the Jewish temple was sacrificing a lamb for the sins of all Israel.

- In dying on the cross, Jesus took upon Himself the sins of all mankind.

He took your place and my place on the cross. He "bore" our sins. He thus became the One who had the capacity to free us and forgive us. Jesus is not "a savior" but *the* Savior, the only One who became a sin-free, substitutionary sacrifice. He alone, as the Son of God, is capable of doing God's work of total forgiveness from sin.

But to be forgiven, a person must believe. And what must be "believed" is very specific—a person must believe that Jesus is the Savior!

What more must be done beyond believing? Nothing. At least not to be saved and receive forgiveness and eternal life. Over and over, Jesus told us, "Only believe."

Jesus reminded His Jewish audience about a time in the history of the Israelites when they were wandering in the wilderness and began to experience a great plague of poisonous vipers. The Lord commanded Moses to fashion a bronze serpent and place it high on a pole in the midst of the Israelite camp with the instructions that all who believed God and *looked* at the serpent would live. In order to enter the Salvation stage, a person needs *only believe*. Nothing could be simpler. Nothing could be more accessible to every person. Nothing could be less cumbersome. The Lord was disciplining the Israelites who were grumbling about their lot: lack of food, water, and a miserable wilderness. The Lord sent fiery serpents who bit and killed many Israelites. Moses interceded with the Lord on their behalf.

Paul wrote to the Ephesians, "For by grace you have been saved through faith, and that not of yourselves; it is the gift of God, not of works, lest anyone should boast" (Ephesians 2:8–9 NKJV). No amount of good works, good personality, or good giving can result in a person moving from Seeking to Salvation—in other words, God does not grade on a "curve" based on man's efforts or human character traits. Salvation cannot be earned or bought. The flip side of this is that there is nothing a person must do beyond believing in order to be saved. Faith is all that is required; and nothing but faith can trigger salvation.

Believing Is Required

Let me make it very clear, however, that believing *is* required.

There are many today who teach that one does not need to actively and intentionally believe in Jesus as Savior in order to enter heaven for all eternity. They believe that every person who has been created after the death of Jesus on the cross has been automatically saved—in other words, to be born is to automatically be heaven-bound. Other closely related beliefs arise from this central belief: there are many paths to heaven, all of them equal; God will not refuse any person entrance to heaven; and there is no need for a person to be converted to Christ if some other religious pathway is preferred by that person for whatever reason. Such beliefs are not in alignment with the total teaching of Jesus and the New Testament writers. The New Testament clearly and repeatedly calls upon a person to take an active, willful, and intentional step of belief. To believe is to receive; to receive is to believe. Jesus said, "Whoever *believes* in Him should not perish but have everlasting life" (John 3:16 NKJV).

I marvel at what the gospel writer John said about Jesus as the free, pure gift of God: "He was in the world, and the world was made through Him, and the world did not know Him. He came to His own, and His own did not receive Him. But *as many as received Him*, to them He gave the right to become children of God, to those who believe on His name: who were born, not of blood, nor of the will of the flesh, nor of the will of man, but of God" (John 1:10–13). God's will is to freely give the gift of membership in His eternal family to those who actively and intentionally receive.

We each bear full responsibility for settling the matter for ourselves. Nobody can be converted on our behalf. No other human being can secure our salvation for us. Seekers must answer these questions for themselves:

- Do I continue to reject the teachings of Christ and the New Testament?

- Do I continue to attempt to resolve all things by myself?

- Can I save myself, have a life hereafter, be with those who have passed on and whom I love?

- Do I yield my life to Christ and allow Him to live within me, transforming me to His likeness?

A person who feels guilt for sin and separation from God, and hears the message that Jesus is the Savior, feels the Holy Spirit's convicting power inside him, and accepts and believes that Jesus is his Savior . . . *is* saved.

What a miracle that is!

Our Salvation Is Secured

Once a person has "believed and received" Jesus as Savior, the Holy Spirit "seals the deal." The apostle Paul wrote to the believers in Ephesus:

> *In Him you also trusted, after you heard the word of truth, the gospel of your salvation; in whom also, having believed, you were sealed with the Holy Spirit of promise, who is the guarantee of our inheritance until the redemption of the purchased posses-sion, to the praise of his glory.*

(EPHESIANS 1:13–14 NKJV)

Salvation is the final result of the spiritual birthing process. Jesus said to a religious leader of His day, Nicodemus, "Unless one is born again, he cannot see the kingdom of God" (John 3:3). When Nico-demus questioned how this could occur, Jesus replied, "Most assur-edly, I say to you, unless one is born of water and the Spirit, he cannot enter the kingdom of God. That which is born of the flesh is flesh, and that which is born of the Spirit is spirit. Do not marvel that I say to you, 'You must be born again.' The wind blows where it wishes, and you hear the sound of it, but cannot tell where it comes from and where it goes. So is everyone who is born of the Spirit" (John 3:5–8).

Jesus spoke of a birthing process, specifically naming water and the Spirit. Certainly the metaphor to physical birth is a strong one. We each at our birth had our beginning in a watery womb and came into this world in a rush of water (or were lifted out of the waters in the case of caesarean births). We immediately began to breathe in oxygen—with a failure to do so bringing about death.

To the Jewish person, these words had added meaning. Going into waters and coming up out of waters was a normal part of ritualistic cleansing for a righteous Jew. Nicodemus, as a religious leader in Je-rusalem, routinely went into a baptismal-style pool of water prior to entering the Temple for worship purposes. To go into the waters was a matter of the *will*. It referred to an intentional, purposeful desire to be cleansed—it was an expression that the person was leaving behind sinful deeds and the sinfulness of the world at large, and was making a new commitment to obedience and right living before God. For Jesus to say that a person must be "born of water" is not necessarily the establishment of a command to be baptized—although some religious denominations claim it to be just that—but in the larger sense, it is a statement that a person's *will* is involved.

A person *wills* to believe—a person chooses to use his faith. Belief is a choice. A person *wills* to receive Christ as a step in faith. We accept or deny Him. We are for or against. Think of it this way: We believe in electricity but no one has ever seen it. But we all "experience" it daily, right? In the same way, and in turn, we experience God. God does not have to prove Himself to His children. Some would say they've never "seen" Him. I can see His hand everywhere.

Einstein, in his last years, was trying to prove God. He could not do it. No one ever will. His final words on earth were, "Find out about prayer." These words were caught by a person who put his ear to the great man's mouth. I believe that he must have recognized that people can experience God, see Him, hear Him, even if they cannot *prove* His existence.

When a person makes the choice or decision to believe, the Spirit immediately indwells that person. It is as if the person opens the door and the Spirit immediately comes in. Jesus said, "Behold, I stand at the door and knock. If anyone hears My voice and opens the door, I will come in to him and dine with him, and he with Me" (Revelation 3:20 NKJV). Jesus indwells us through His Holy Spirit.

Wishing is not willing. If we must be filled with the Holy Spirit and are willing to pay the price that may be required, we will be filled with the Spirit. Jesus did not wish to die on the cross but He was willing. "Nevertheless, Your will, not mine." Fear and doubt are two of Satan's top weapons. Think about it: I'd bet that every decision you have ever made—which in the end was driven by fear or doubt after reason gave you a different answer—has turned out to be the wrong one. For it was against the ultimate authority of our Lord. Reason said, "Do it." Fear said, "Better not." And so we never got out of the starting gate. If we are Spirit-filled we will step out in faith. God will support our efforts when they are within His will. Then we cannot fail.

This willful receiving of Jesus—believing He is the Savior—and the resulting immediate indwelling of the Spirit results in a *state of being* that the Church from its inception has called "Salvation." A person is "saved" from sin in two ways:

First, Salvation refers to a state of *total spiritual cleansing from all past sin*. The person is set free—fully forgiven, and released from all guilt and shame associated with sin. No matter how horrendous the sins a person may have committed—no matter how fierce the rebellion against God—the slate is wiped clean by God as an act of His mercy and love. This does not mean that certain consequences of prior sin will cease to be in effect on the person's *flesh*—the wages of sin produce physical death. (Thus, a saved adulterer might still have a social disease; a saved alcoholic might still have a corroded liver; a saved abuser might still have broken relationships.) It does mean, however, that any consequences of prior sin on the person's *spirit* are totally eliminated. (Regardless of what has transpired before, transformation inside has now occurred—giving a person total healing on the inside, despite any "flesh" consequences.) The person receives the gift of eternal life from the moment of believing, and such a gift, given by the Giver of all good gifts, is never revoked (see James 1:16–18).

Second, salvation refers to a *"redemption" from Satan's control and sin's power*. In the ancient world, slaves were routinely bought and sold in slave markets. A slave that was "redeemed" was a slave that was purchased, and then set free by the person who made the purchase. A redeemed slave was no longer in "bondage"—he or she was given a new identity. The person no longer was required to give *any* form of service to a former master, or even to acknowledge that he had once belonged to another person. All legal, financial, and material shackles on the person's life were broken at the moment of redemption. In like manner, when a person believes and receives Jesus as Savior, Jesus "redeems" that person from the slave status the person has had to the devil and to sin. The person is freed from the bondage of sinfulness, and is given the ability, by the indwelling power of the Holy Spirit, to say no to temptation. All spiritual shackles are broken from the person's life—Satan never again has claim to that person's eternal spirit. He may still harass, depress, impress, and oppress a person in this life, but he has no power or authority to possess that person eternally.

When my wife Ginny was ill with cancer but still feeling well, she was downstairs watching a situation comedy and I was upstairs in bed, praying. She was laughing heartily. Suddenly I heard the coldest, iciest voice I had ever heard. It said, "Your wife is going to die." I replied without hesitation, "I know who you are, Satan! At the name of Jesus every knee must bow, including yours. Leave me now and never return." What was Satan up to? Trying to stop me from fulfilling His purpose for my life. He spoke the truth, of course, since Ginny was fighting a terminal disease—but he was using fear and doubt as his weapons to drive me back from my cause. Had I listened to Satan, this book would not have been written. Incidentally, the Devil has never come back.

What a glorious and wondrous thing salvation is! Man's will and the Spirit's indwelling are the source of the life our Lord promised us (the joyous, hundred-life) on this earth and in eternity. In less time than can be measured, a person is "birthed" spiritually. He is made totally and completely "new."

Just as a baby physically birthed cannot return to the watery womb, so a person who is spiritually birthed cannot revert to a former state of sinfulness. The baby becomes a resident of a "new world" complete with gravity, atmosphere, physical sensations, and separation from mother. The spiritual baby also enters a "new world"— one framed by God's commands and empowered by the Spirit. In a similar way, the saved person is separated from the clutch of the enemy and the bondage of sin.

Having been indwelled by God's Holy Spirit, the new "believer" in Christ has been "converted." He has been birthed. He has entered a new realm—a new life, a new set of possibilities and responsibilities. As we look at the Path of Life model, very specifically, the person cannot revert to a state of Sleeping or merely Seeking. The door to those stages is closed.

Conversion, while definitive with regard to the past, marks only the "starting point" for the spiritual transformation that lies ahead.

The Beating of a Living Heart

One of the most beautiful metaphors in the Bible relates to Conversion. It is at Conversion that a person begins to live spiritually. Prior to that time, a person may have had a healthy physical heart—but spiritually speaking, the person had a dead heart, a heart of stone. The heart, of course, relates to the *spiritual will* of a person, not to a person's emotions. Prior to conversion, a person has no spiritual will that is "alive" to God's purposes. Rather, the person has only the will to ignore God's plan and walk apart from God's presence.

Long before Jesus came, the prophet Ezekiel gave this prophetic message: "I will give you a new heart and put a new spirit within you . . . I will cause you to walk in my statutes and you will keep my judgments and do *them*" (Ezekiel 36:26–27 NKJV).

Almost a thousand years before Ezekiel, Moses, under the inspiration of the Holy Spirit, called upon the Israelites to return to the Lord, obey Him, be restored, cleansed, and live. He said to them about their ongoing occupation of the land God had promised to them:

> "Return to the Lord your God and obey Him with all your heart and soul according to all that I command you today, you and your sons, then the Lord your God will restore you from captivity and have compassion on you . . . I have set before you your death, the blessing and the curse. So choose life that you may live, you and your descendants. By loving the Lord your God, by obeying His voice, and by Him . . ." (Deuteronomy 30:2,3,19,20 NAST).

Moses quickly pointed out to the Israelites that this command was not too difficult to understand or to perform. Knowing God's will is possible! Keeping God's commands is doable! Moses added that the Lord was not distant—far off in heaven. Nor was He beyond the sea in a manner that a person might need to go fetch God in order to know Him. No! The presence of the Lord was close at hand—as close as their lips and hearts.

The Holy Spirit, as Guardian of God's Word, put the command of God on Moses' lips. He works in like manner with us. He brings God's Word quickly to our minds so we might know it. He drills God's Word deep into our hearts so we might desire to do it. He equips us with His power and strength so that we might actually live it!

The Holy Spirit is called in the creeds of the church "the giver of life." Indeed, it is the Holy Spirit who indwells our hearts at conversion and brings our heart to *life*! We experience new joy, new peace, new desires, new perspective. We become new creatures filled with new *life*. Everything from the point of Conversion onward becomes an exercise in *newness*. The old has passed away. *All* things become new.

ETERNITY

LifeGate 7: Sanctified Service

LifeGate 6: Anointing

LifeGate 5: Surrendering

LifeGate 4: Yielding

LifeGate 3: Converting

LifeGate 2: Seeking

LifeGate 1: Awakening

ASLEEP

Seven LifeGates:
The stairway to the transcendent life in the here and now.

When our Lord said, "Come, follow Me," He meant for
you and me to bring our spiritual selves into harmony,
and ultimately into perfect harmony with Him.
In short, we are to become one:
He in me, I in Him, abiding together, forever.
In so doing, we become fully integrated, "whole" and
eternal persons, dwelling forever in His presence.
This is the purpose of life.

chapter 5

Walking in Newness of Life: Conversion

LifeGate 3

H olograms *have become commonplace in* our world. In a true hologram, a flat image seemingly allows a person to see the object in three dimensions. Turn the hologram and you will "see" around the corner. But if you cut a one-inch hologram in half, it is still all there! You can also cut it in fourths and it is still complete. The image remains, even when it is cut to a microscopic size. In a similar way, the Holy Spirit is everywhere at once. He can orchestrate your life and mine together in harmony with all of the other believers on the earth. He is infinite and yet completely personal to each individual. What an awesome mystery this is!

An equal mystery is this: When we come to Christ, He lives within us in the form of His Holy Spirit—*all* of the Spirit—our soul is God within us. We receive the *fullness* of the Holy Spirit even though very few, if any, of us ever grasp that truth or live in the full reality of His presence at the moment we are converted.

The Holy Spirit gives us *all* that life has to offer us. He makes available to us an abundant life on this earth, and simultaneously, a perfect life that has no end in the glory of God's heavenly presence.

We do not automatically experience *all* of that life. We begin to experience it, walk into it, and as we continue to walk with Christ, we experience more and more of it.

The Holy Spirit imparts to us the *perfection* of Christ Jesus' character likeness. We read about those character qualities in Galatians 5:22–23 where these nine are listed: love, joy, peace, patience, kindness, goodness, faithfulness, gentleness, and self-control. We do not automatically reflect all of those qualities in their perfection, of course. As we mature, or "grow up" and into our faith, we become more and more like Christ Jesus (Ephesians 4:13).

Two Key Questions

There are two key questions I encourage you to ask yourself often: Are you willing to be an Everyday Saint? Are you willing to be alive at the Divine level?

- *Am I Willing to Be a Saint?* Many people shy away from the concept of saintliness. Some do not believe they can be a saint, although God's Word clearly says otherwise. Some believe it is a Roman Catholic concept. It is not at all limited to our Catholic friends. The biblical term is applied to those who have "separated" themselves from the world. Saints are those who are denying their lower fleshly instincts in the pursuit of a higher spiritual purity and calling in Christ.

The greater reality in many cases is that people simply do not *want* to become saints. They do not want to give up self and know the fullness of what it means to be "I in Christ and Christ in me." They do not want to live completely dependent upon God. The saint knows God has a hold on his life and that doing God's will is all that matters.

While bearing a spirit of humility and being stripped of all but one's innocence, the saint feels completely at one with God in the natural world. He has absolute confidence and trust that God is the center of reality. His life is righteous, filled with faith, and completely alive in Christ and dead to the flesh. The saint lives in moment-by-moment relationship with Christ. Indeed, the saint's attitudes, actions, and words are inseparable from those of Christ.

The saint is Spirit-led. Sadly to me, the term "Spirit-led" has been used so loosely that this phrase, for most people, has lost the richness of meaning it rightly deserves. The surrendered soul who lives out Christ's will most definitely will reveal a life of saintliness because it is the Spirit who directs that life and leads that life into a fullness of service.

Saintliness requires the daily practice of faith. It is rooted in an overwhelming desire to please the Lord in all we do—becoming Christ-like in a way that is visible to everyone else. The assumption of Christ's character is paramount, even as we retain our own identity.

Do saints suffer? Oh, yes. No example of sainthood can be found that does not involve suffering. Saints, however, bear the pain and hardships of this earthly life without complaint. They recognize that suffering is part of the refining process that allows them to more fully reflect the glory of the Lord. Neither Debbie or her mother, my wife Ginny, ever complained of their fate.

Even in suffering, a saint remains "confident of this very thing, that He who has begun a good work . . . will perfect it until the day of Jesus Christ" (Philippians 1:6 NASB).

The supreme noteworthy truth about sainthood is that we are *called* by God to be saints.

From the book of Isaiah through the Revelation of John, Scripture has about fifty references to our being "saints." That is the identity to which we each are called—not "saints" in the highly prescribed doctrine of a particular church or denomination, but saints as the early disciples considered themselves to be. Saints are those whose sins have been forgiven and who are daily surrendering their lives to the unfolding will of God.

Let me ask again, "Are you willing to be a saint?"

The Holy Spirit imparts to His saints the ability to think, choose, decide, respond, and understand all things with a deeper mind . . . a mind and soul in fellowship with our Lord, in direct communication (1 John 1:3). He is the spirit of Truth. He imparts all that we need to know to live a Godly life. He is our wise counselor who testifies of Christ and gives us the ability to think as Jesus thought, feel as Jesus felt, and speak and act as Jesus spoke and acted. Paul informs us in Corinthians 6:17, "But the one who joins himself to the Lord is one spirit with Him" (NAST). Those abilities, however, do not emerge in us full-blown at the moment of our conversion. Paul wrote to the Romans: "And do not be conformed to this world but be transformed by the renewing of your mind, that you may prove what is that good and acceptable and perfect will of God" (Romans 12:2 NAST).

Oswald Chambers was the son of a pastor. As a youth, he preferred the ways of the world rather than God's and was in open rebellion. As he matured he came to think, "Maybe I have ahold of the wrong end of the stick." Our Lord continued to nudge him until he yielded—and fully embraced his conversion. I've read all of his published works; he sensed that he would be a bright flame, burning for a short time—and he was right. He died at age forty-three. In his classic devotional, *My Utmost for His Highest*, he speaks about *surrender* in about 80 percent of the devotions, a key aspect of conversion and living the fullest, richest Christian life (we'll get into that in a later chapter). I have no better example of a Spirit-filled life than his.

Every area of our life is permeated by the Holy Spirit at the moment of our Conversion; it's a lot like a sponge, absorbing more and more water. It's His work to bring us to wholeness—fully functioning, in harmony in all aspects of our being, and completely developed.

We are one being—with spiritual, emotional, intellectual, and physical facets to our personhood. In our western civilization, we tend to isolate these areas of mind, emotions, spirit, and body for analysis, examining each of these aspects of personhood as if these categories occur naturally. In truth, a person cannot be divided in this way.

You cannot tell about your spiritual life without describing what you feel and think. You cannot express what you think without revealing to a certain degree how you feel. All expressed thoughts and feelings reveal something about your spiritual state. It is as if you and I are multifaceted cut diamonds, each facet capturing a radiating degree of light. Even so, all facets are part of the same stone.

A person's spiritual state is the ultimate influence over all other facets of that person's life—even if that person does not think of himself as being "spiritual" and even if the person does not acknowledge the centrality of the spirit to his total being. The spirit is the everlasting essence of our being—the overriding ruler of every relationship and the integrating force of the "I." When the spirit is tuned to self, self-centeredness is pervasive. Thoughts and emotions cause us to relate to others and to the physical and material world in self-absorbing ways.

On the other hand, when the spirit is tuned to God through the saving grace of Jesus Christ and the indwelling of God's Holy Spirit, Christ-centeredness becomes pervasive. Our thoughts are no less directed, our emotions are no less ruled. Our relationships are no less impacted and the relationship between the physical and material world is no less important. What is different is that the *influence* of the Spirit upon these other aspects of personhood is 180 degrees opposite that of a self-centered spirit.

And that brings us to the second question we must frequently ask ourselves:

- *Am I Willing to Live at the Divine Level?* When we are transformed, and our spiritual focus moves us from self-centeredness to Christ-centeredness, we truly become *new creatures*. We are new beings in our totality! It is not merely our spirit that is changed, but our entire being is changed. Our responses, desires, goals, thoughts, feelings, purchases, and physical concerns undergo a radical change the longer we walk with Christ Jesus. We come to the place where we're just as comfortable talking about spiritual matters as we are about the latest movie we saw, the most recent book we read, or the item we have just purchased. Some of us undergo radical change within weeks of salvation. Independent of rate of change, everyone undergoes ongoing change following salvation.

This work of re-creation, of renewal, of "making whole," is the work of the Holy Spirit, the Lord, the giver of *life*. We cannot do the work on our own. He is the Author and the Finisher of the work and our part is to yield to Him as Master Instructor. He enables us to go where He directs. He empowers us to do what He commands. He instructs us to know what He requires us to understand and convey. Whatever the Spirit compels us to do, He equips us to do. The first disciples could not believe they could accomplish their mission. The Spirit equipped them. This is why Christianity is the force it is today.

The Agent of Transformation

The Holy Spirit is the agent of our transformation and transcendence to living on the Divine level. In the original language in which it was written, the phrase "be transformed" in Romans 12:2 is in the present, active tense—it is neither past nor future, it is *now*. We are works in progress *today*. We are *being transformed* right now . . . and in the next moment, and in the next and the next. To the Lord, each of us is a wondrous work and His transforming work is ongoing and lovingly performed. It is popular thinking to "live in the now." This was Jesus' advice to us thousands of years ago.

Billy Graham's son, Franklin, had a difficult time growing up. At one point Billy said, "If he wants to break my heart, he is going about it the right way." But unconditional love and continual prayer gave us the Franklin Graham that we know today. The Spirit transformed Franklin as He did my adopted son, Bill.

We adopted Bill at age four—one of three children we adopted after Debbie died. I was forty-five at the time. Several adoption agencies turned us down saying it wouldn't work, not at our age. We were living in Valley Forge, Pennsylvania, and one day there was a telephone call from the Children's Aid Society. "You have asked for two children . . . [we had thought that one might somehow be thought of as a replacement] . . . and you have refused to take no as an answer. What would you say to three? They have one mother, by two fathers. They are four, six, and eight." Ginny and I said yes. With the adoption we were back to four children at home; Ginny emerged from her depression and was a fully functioning mother and wife once more. Billy had been wrecked by a terrible foster home; he was left in a highchair to feed himself, often in a soiled diaper. He became a very, very angry child.

In our home he got nothing but unconditional love. As he got older, his behavior was abominable. He broke into homes for drug money and fell deeper and deeper into drugs. We sought help and the consensus said that Billy needed to be in a psychiatric hospital. So Billy spent a year and a half in the hospital. At that point Blue Cross refused to pay any longer and we could not afford the $5,000 per month cost. When Billy came home he immediately resumed stealing and breaking into neighbors' homes. He said it gave him a "high." One night he got up after we put him to bed and went out to break into a neighbor's home. The neighbor apprehended him and held a .45 revolver to his head. "My God! You're our neighbor's son." This landed him in prison for two years. Ginny cried as the judge told us what rotten parents we were. I asked her, "If we are so rotten why are Carol and Kathie okay?" The judge didn't know what he was talking about.

What saved Billy was God's unconditional love. That's the healing force, and it took Billy finding God to find healing. Today Billy is a great husband and father, and has a fine pool maintenance business.

You can become an Everyday Saint. You might be muttering right now, "Me, an emerging saint? You have to be kidding!" But the *reality* is that when we allow the Holy Spirit to do His Divine work in us, transcendence is not at all difficult. Obedience is easy because it is born of intense love, not duty. Duty is burdensome. Love is joyous (see Matthew 11:30). The Holy Spirit is not a domineering taskmaster, but a loving Counselor and Comforter who desires our eternal best.

Our part is to love the Lord and out of our love, to obey the Spirit's promptings within us. His part is to transform us into the character likeness of Christ Jesus!

The Holy Spirit does the work!

- He guards the Word of God within us—sealing it in our minds so that it becomes a part of our thought process (Nehemiah 9:20).

- He restores us to the Father (Psalms 51:10).

- He imparts to us the nature—the character—of Christ (Galatians 5:22–25).

- He is with us always through our life journey—teaching, comforting, encouraging, empowering, bringing to remembrance and enabling us to overcome all manner of evil and temptation (John 14:26).

- He directs the accomplishment of God's purpose for us—in the same manner as He directed Jesus throughout His earthly life (Matthew 28:19, 20).

It is wonderful to gain perspective on just how the Holy Spirit worked in the life of Jesus. It was the Holy Spirit who was the source of the virgin birth in Mary (Matthew 3:13–15). The Holy Spirit was evident at the baptism of Jesus on the shores of the Jordan River (Matthew 3:16, 17). The Holy Spirit was with Jesus in the wilderness, helping Him resist the temptations of Satan (Matthew 4:1). It was the Holy Spirit who fulfilled the prophecy of Isaiah that a Messiah, through His power, would "proclaim liberty to the captives," and which Jesus quotes in Luke 4:18. It was by the power of the Holy Spirit that Jesus healed the sick, calmed the storms, and cast out demons (Matthew 12:28).

While the doctrine of the Trinity was not fully disclosed until Jesus came, God paved the way in the Old Testament with about eighty references to the Spirit and the coming of a Messiah. For example,

Daniel (Daniel 7:13 NASB) states, "I kept looking in the night visions, and behold, with the clouds of heaven *One like* a Son of Man was coming . . ." Jesus Himself used the name to indicate that He was the incarnate Son of God. The use of the word "like" is to indicate that the Son of Man is the perfect model of humanity while not being a man in the human sense.

In Daniel 7:14, *Him* refers to the Son of Man who will reign over all things as God's regent. There are many references in the New Testament that His Kingdom will be everlasting. As Jesus prepared His disciples for His return to heaven, He told them, "And I will ask the Father, and He will give you another helper, that He may be with you forever; that is the Spirit of truth . . ." (John 14:16–17 NASB). Prior to Jesus coming the Spirit was active on earth, but after Jesus went home, the Helper (the Spirit) came to permanently indwell all believers.

There is total harmony between the Old and New Testaments:

1. The Old Testament forecasts the coming of the Lord of Lords, the King of Kings.

2. Jesus, Son of Man, is born. (New Testament)

3. When He goes home, a Helper, the Spirit, comes as Jesus said He would. (New Testament)

In our lives today it is the Holy Spirit who enables us to live out the great Commission of Christ—to go and make disciples of all nations (Matthew 28:18–19). It is the Holy Spirit who is the source of all spiritual truth and discernment (1 Corinthians 2:13, 15). It is the Holy Spirit who gives us spiritual gifts (1 Corinthians 12:1, 3, 4, 7, 11, and Romans 12:4–8). It is the Holy Spirit who develops unity and community in the Body of Christ—both privately and publicly (John 4:24). It is the Holy Spirit who anoints us for our particular roles in the Body of Christ (Acts 10:38).

Through the Spirit of Christ abiding in us, we are truly more than conquerors of life's trials and tribulations. We cannot fail in doing those things He has planned for us to accomplish. When we surrender, we are already in the "win" column! It is the Holy Spirit who secures the victory. We simply need to walk the path that He has set before us, trusting in His power for the courage we need to walk!

So many people try to be "good" or to "get good" on their own after their conversion to Christ. It is impossible!

I love the words of Matthew 11:28–30: "Come to Me, all who are weary and heavy-laden, and I will give you rest. Take My yoke upon you and learn from Me, for I am gentle and humble in heart; and you shall find rest for your souls. *For My yoke is easy, and My burden is light.*"

What a wonderful invitation! The work of the Holy Spirit is a gentle, peace-creating work within us. He instructs, guides, comforts, and encourages us gently, as a patient parent teaching a child.

The Freedoms Given to Us by the Spirit

We are indwelled by the Holy Spirit but we are not imprisoned, nor are we possessed by the Spirit. The Holy Spirit always allows for the free will of the person and for the free expression of a person's *creativity, personality*, and *initiative*. What the Holy Spirit does impart to us by His indwelling is an *ability* to act in a way that brings out our potential and causes us to grow into the fullness of who God initially designed us to be.

Using myself as an example, I can see progressive movement in me to become more like my Lord. I used to use language while leading groups that I would not consider using today. As I have said, I have not been drunk ever since I accepted God as my Savior. If this had not happened, I would probably not be alive.

Very specifically, the Spirit imparts to us three "abilities" to use as we choose to use them. They are at the core of our freedom in Christ. It is the Spirit who makes it possible for a person to confess Christ, to repent, and to put off a former life and simultaneously take on a new life. Let me briefly touch upon these three aspects of "potentiality" that belong to the new believer because of the Holy Spirit's presence in his life.

Confession

To confess Christ is to say, in Paul's terms, "I am in Christ and Christ is in me." Paul wrote this to the Romans:

> *If you confess with your mouth the Lord Jesus and believe in your heart that God has raised Him from the dead, you shall be saved; for with the heart man believes, resulting in righteous-ness, and with the mouth he confesses resulting in salvation. For the Scripture says, "Whoever believes in Him will not be dis-appointed." . . . For the same Lord is Lord of all, abounding in riches for all who call upon Him; For "whoever will call on the name of the Lord shall be saved."*

(ROMANS 10:9–13 NAST)

The confession of the believer is very important for several reasons. It is important so that all emotional and "identity" shackles that have entrapped a person's mind and heart might be broken. It is in proclaiming, "I am in Christ and Christ is in me" that a person truly comes to accept his own salvation. Chants help embed truth. *I am in Christ and Christ is in Me.* As part of our devotions, prayers, and meditation, this helps Christ to indwell us. As I have written, the Spirit does not want to possess or imprison us. If our Lord wanted robots he would not have created us in His image. A Christian psy-chologist who helped me immensely through a difficult period taught me to go to one of my conference rooms, tell my secretaries I was not to be disturbed, and to repeat for five minutes, "Happy, healthy, holy am I." Five minutes later I was calm, not fretting. Try adding, "I am in Christ and Christ is in me" to your time in prayer. See what happens. My sister Janet recently said to me: "Tommy, you do not worry." She is the only one in the world who calls me by my growing up name. And I told her, "You are right, I do not worry." This is the result of my surrender. It is peace of soul. It is understanding that Christ is in me—and if He's not worried, neither am I.

Many times people have said to me, "I believe in Jesus and have received Him, but I am still haunted by my memories of past sin. I still feel guilty and ashamed." The solution for these people lies in the realm of confession. They need to say to themselves and to others, "I am in Christ and Christ is in me." The truth of this statement is the key to their beginning to experience a genuine transformation of the mind so they can take on the identity of Christ-follower and Christ-server. Psychologists call this imprinting. We are willing ourselves to be Christ-like.

For years I have helped clients make transformations in behavior, mind, and beliefs, by making cue cards of what they want. I use them for myself. This is one . . . it concerns speech. "I resolve that every word I ever speak will be a blessing, never a curse." A joke at someone else's expense is a curse, not a blessing. In the eastern states of our country there are the so-called West Virginia jokes. I have stopped grandchildren from telling them. They put a whole people down. Jokes about Jews do the same. I have had executives keep cue cards just out of sight during a meeting, for example, on their lap while sitting at their desk. The idea is to cue themselves, to remember the goal of becoming a bit more like Christ.

Why does Paul call upon the believer to believe that God raised Jesus from the dead? Because the resurrection of Christ was the central fact to the early church that Jesus was and is GOD. It is the definitive statement the early church made about the divinity of Jesus. It *made* Him the Messiah—the anointed one who was the rightful ruler of God's people. We believe Jesus is the Messiah with our will-activated faith (this kind of faith was the Jewish understanding of the word "heart") . . . but it is as we conform our own minds and emotions that we begin to live a Christ-centered life. It is the *con-*

fession of our mouth that shifts our focus away from self and toward Christ. It is the *confession* of our mouth that allows others to identify us as a Christ-follower. We are out of the closet. This is why a person joining a church is asked questions that require positive answers.

The confession "I in Christ and Christ in me" is a confession that we are in an eternal relationship with Jesus Christ. We are reconciled. Jesus said that when we confess Him before others in this manner on earth, He confesses His relationship with us before the angels in heaven. Jesus said, "Everyone therefore who shall confess Me before men, him I will also confess before My Father who is in heaven" (Matthew 10:32). In other words, when we say, "I in Christ and Christ in me," Jesus simultaneously declares to His Father, "I am in that person and that person is in Me!"

We also must recognize that it is the Holy Spirit in us that makes possible both our initial and our ongoing confession of Christ. One *cannot* proclaim, "I in Christ and Christ in me" apart from the Holy Spirit! Paul wrote to the believers in Corinth, "No one speaking by the Spirit of God says Jesus' accursed; and no one can say that Jesus is Lord except by the Holy Spirit" (1 Corinthians 12:3). The Bible also tells us, "And I will ask the Father and he will give you another helper, that he may be with you forever. He abides with you, and will be in you (John 4:16, 17 NAST). He does not ever depart.

Repentance

The Holy Spirit makes it possible for a person to repent. To repent is to "turn around." It is to change direction, to alter one's course through life *away* from sin and disobedience and *toward* righteousness and obedience. To repent is to say, "I will no longer sin" and to say instead, "I will choose to obey."

President Reagan had virtually nothing but opposition on his "Evil Empire" speech. He refused to change his thoughts. Years after the Soviet collapse, at a dinner between Soviet and U.S. arms negotiators, there was discussion of what caused its collapse. A former senior Soviet general proclaimed, "You know what caused the collapse of the Soviet Union? You know what did it?" he shouted. "That damned speech about the evil empire! That's what did it." Standing, he added: "It was an evil empire. It was!"

President Reagan acted with a Christ-perspective. He had read a Christian novel when he was eleven and thereafter became a devout Christian, remaining so throughout sixty years of public service.*

Jesus repeatedly called the Holy Spirit the "Helper"—the One called alongside to counsel us as the Spirit of Truth and to enable us to pursue the truth once revealed to our hearts. He points to the truth and empowers a truth-based life. The Spirit helps us to shun sin and to both *seek* and to *live out* the Christ-centered life.

Repentance is a choice, and once we have believed and received Christ, the Holy Spirit enables us to make *Godly* choices. The Spirit illuminates the Scripture to us so that we truly understand what we read in God's Word. He gives us insight into how to apply God's Word, and thus live in wisdom. The Spirit gives us the ability to discern right from wrong, and to discern the work of the enemy of our souls (discernment of evil spirits) and the work of God and His chosen vessels. He gives us the ability to understand what God wants us to do and become.

Every day, each of us is required to make countless decisions—most of them dealing with issues and relationships and choices that either move us closer to God or farther away from God. We perhaps do not think of some of these behavior acts as "decisions," but they are decisions nonetheless. *What* we say to a spouse, child, friend, coworker, client, patient, employer, vendor, customer, or stranger is a decision. *How* we speak—the volume and tone we use and the body language we display—is a matter of choice. *When* we speak and to *whom* we speak are choices. *Where* we go and *what* we do are choices. We must "decide" whether we will act out of self or with a Christ-perspective.

---

* Paul Kenger, *God and Ronald Reagan* (New York: HarperCollins, 2004), p. 259.

Repentance, therefore, is not a one-time act, just as confession is not a one-time statement. We confess, "Christ in me and I in Christ" as often as we need to be reminded of our relationship with Him! We repent—making choices away from Satan and sin and toward Christ and righteous obedience on a minute-by-minute, hour-by-hour, day-by-day basis.

Putting on the New Man

Paul wrote to the believers in Ephesus:

> *The truth is in Jesus: that you put off, concerning your former conduct, the old man which grows corrupt according to the deceitful lusts, and be renewed in the spirit of your mind, and that you put on the new man which was created according to God, in true righteousness and holiness.*

> (EPHESIANS 4:21–24 NKJV)

Paul went on to tell the Ephesians very specific *behaviors* that they needed to put off and to put on. He insisted that they give up lying, ungodly anger, stealing, laziness, corrupt words, bitterness, wrath, clamor, evil speaking, malice, fornication, uncleanness, covetousness, filthiness, foolish talking, coarse jesting, and all deceitfulness (see Ephesians 4:25–31; 5:3–5). In other writings he insisted that they display no "works of the flesh" including adultery, lewdness, idolatry, sorcery, hatred, arguments, jealousies, outbursts of wrath, selfish ambitions, disagreements, ungodly beliefs, envy, murders, drunkenness, and anything that would alienate one believer from another (see Galatians 5:19–21). Furthermore they were not even to associate with those who were "sons of disobedience" and not to be "partakers with them" of such behaviors (see Ephesians 5:6–7).

If parents have a "follower" child they need to pay close attention to whom they befriend. Followers have a great need to be popular. If they fall in with the wrong crowd they are prone to get in trouble, and partake of bad behaviors.

Paul told the first-century believers to put on kindness and to be "tenderhearted, forgiving one another, even as God in Christ forgave you" (Ephesians 4:32 NKJV). He challenged the believers to "walk as children of light" and to display the character qualities of the Holy Spirit who dwelt within them: goodness, righteousness, and truth. They were to live their lives with deeds marked by the flowing from an inner character of love, joy, peace, long-suffering, kindness, faithfulness, gentleness, and self-control (see Ephesians 5:8–9 and Galatians 5:22–23).

Certainly these passages do not provide an exhaustive list of all the behaviors that the "saved" person is to put off or put on. What these passages point to is this: The Holy Spirit produces in us a new way of living! Our willful exercise of the great freedoms bestowed by the Holy Spirit releases the Spirit's work:

- *In confession*, the Holy Spirit prompts us to adopt a new attitude, perspective, and worldview. The Holy Spirit works in us to "save" us from our old way of thinking and feeling. The Holy Spirit empowers us to confess that we are in Christ. He enables us to develop a Christ-centered identity.

- *In repentance*, the Holy Spirit guides us in our decision making and choice making. He leads us into the paths of righteousness—morally right, virtuous, honorable.

- *In enabling us to put off the old man and put on the new man*, the Holy Spirit empowers us to develop new habits and to adopt a new lifestyle that is Godly and in perfect alignment with God's love and law.

All of these things—which cover the full spectrum of what we think, feel, and do—are made available to us, beginning at this stage of Conversion. The Holy Spirit seals us as Christ's own forever. He sets up residence in us with the intent of developing us into the full character likeness of Jesus Christ.

So many Christians seem to think that the Holy Spirit helps them "get saved" and then, for some mysterious reason, the Holy Spirit disappears and the person is pretty much "on her own" to walk through the rest of her life until the moment she dies and goes to heaven. Nothing could be further from the full teaching of the New Testament. The Holy Spirit indwells us at the moment we believe and receive Jesus as Savior—it is at that moment that the Holy Spirit truly becomes active in us to refine us and change us.

Does the Enemy Depart Completely?

The Enemy never departs completely. Our battle against evil does not end with conversion. To the contrary! The real battle begins at that point. Conversion is like the sounding gun for an intense battle between the person's carnal nature and spiritual nature. Think of a battlefield; if new troops arrive, the enemy instantly is on the alert. When the spirit comes alive, the enemy immediately engages in an active battle to make the fledgling believer ineffective. He launches an all-scale attack to steal, kill, and destroy all effectiveness of the "baby Christian." Satan cannot undo salvation—that work is fully accomplished and sealed—but Satan makes every effort to make the "confessing, repenting, and putting off and putting on" aspects of salvation null and void.

What Changes Are Expected?

The degree and types of change in each person's life vary according to that person's prior behavior. The bottom line for *all* people, however, is this: *change is expected*. None of us lives a perfect life prior to Conversion. None of us lives a perfect life even after Conversion. The

Holy Spirit's perfecting work in us is a work of "change" from what was imperfect to what is perfect—working on us our whole lives.

A minister once gave this illustration about the before-and-after nature of conversion. He declared, "There is a marked change *in behavior* that comes with conversion" and then he led his congregation to take a piece of paper and draw a line down the center of the page. He asked the congregation to head the lefthand column "Before Christ," and to label the righthand column "After Christ." He then asked the group assembled, "What's different?"

He admonished the group to identify only those things that they knew from personal experience, external or internal, to be markedly different in their lives preconversion and postconversion.

Nobody in this group of about a hundred people moved to write anything on their papers. Several looked with puzzlement at the minister. Some looked furtively to the left and right to see what others around them may have written. Nobody had written anything!

The reason? While everybody in the room claimed to have received Jesus as their personal Savior through an act of believing, none of them had actively engaged in confessing Christ, repenting, or putting off the old nature and putting on a new one. They had accepted Christ and the freedoms given them by the Holy Spirit, but they were not living as spiritually free people.

Finally one woman in the front row bowed her head and quickly scribbled something on her paper. The minister asked if she would be willing to share what she had written. She handed the minister her paper. Under the heading "Before Christ" were these words: "no hope of eternal life." Under "After Christ" she had written: "some hope."

One man in the group asked the minister, "What should be the differences?" The minister offered the twenty-two categories listed below. I invite you to engage in the exercise for yourself.

Anger management
Conflict resolution
Decision making

Addressing worry
Confronting fear
Submitting to authority
Expressing sexuality
Acquiring self-esteem
Dealing with family relationships
Feeling inner peace
Managing money
Managing time
Choosing entertainment
Supervising/leading others
Spending time with God (prayer)
Establishing priorities
Setting goals
Getting involved in church
Witnessing for Christ
Showing compassion for others
Reading/studying the Bible
Meditation

Others:

The key question is this: What are the before-Christ and after-Christ attributes of *your* life?

Fill out the chart. If you do this once a year, in time you will see how God is transforming you.

Name _____

Date First Done _____

My Attributes	Before Conversion to Christ	After Conversion to Christ
Example: *Anger management*	*Tendency to explode*	*Calmer*
_____	_____	_____
_____	_____	_____
_____	_____	_____
_____	_____	_____
_____	_____	_____
_____	_____	_____
_____	_____	_____
_____	_____	_____
_____	_____	_____
_____	_____	_____
_____	_____	_____
_____	_____	_____
_____	_____	_____
_____	_____	_____
_____	_____	_____

One man in the minister's congregation spoke up and said, "You mean to say that there should be a difference in the way we deal with each of these areas after we become Christians?" He was dumbfounded at the concept.

Same Ol', Same Ol'

In truth, many people who claim they are Christians, and who say that Jesus is their Savior, cannot point to any *real* behavioral or attitudinal changes in their lives preconversion and postconversion. They go to the same places "after Christ" that they've always gone, do the things they've always done, talk the same as everybody else (including an occasional profane word for punctuation); they drink just as much alcohol and take just as many antacid, anti-anxiety, and stimulant concoctions and medications to adjust their moods and motivational levels; see the same kinds of movies; read the same kinds of books as they did "BC"—before Christ. They admit privately, if not publicly, that they still have deep unresolved doubts, fears, worries, and anxieties. They divorce at the same rate and have marital and parenting problems to the same degree. They have very little if any inner peace beyond what they had before. They struggle greatly with the same temptations and continue to make the same mistakes and have the same regrets.

Only about a third of those who claim to be "spiritually reborn" attend church regularly. A much lower percentage tithe (give 10 percent of their income to the church). A very low percentage of church members are involved in the ministries of any church group—and certainly an extremely low percentage remain involved year after year. Numerous polls confirm these conclusions.

So what's different? Very little in the case of most of the "converted."

"Stuck" in Salvation

Countless Christians live at the Salvation stage for the rest of their lives. This is not because the Holy Spirit has ceased to work in the person's life. It is because the person chooses *not to respond* to the Holy Spirit's "still small voice" speaking deep within.

Very specifically, a person does not move beyond Salvation because he chooses *not to confess* Christ when the Holy Spirit prompts the person to confess Christ. To confess Christ is to acknowledge one's belief in Christ as Lord. Many people fall silent in matters of religion. They do not stand as a witness to their faith. The Holy Spirit will not force a person to speak or to act. He inspires, convicts, prompts, urges, and as a friend of mine says, "pushes and prods," but He does not insist or demand that we actually speak or act. The indwelling of the Spirit always honors the person's free will of choice. (This distinguishes the indwelling of the Holy Spirit from the "possessing" quality of Satan in a dramatic way. When Satan possesses a person, that person cries out and behaves uncontrollably—apart from human will. The Satan-possessed person is manipulated and used totally for Satan's purposes, without any regard to the dignity or free will of the person.)

The Spirit-led person is Spirit-filled. Those who are stuck at the Conversion Gate do not understand what it means to be Spirit-led. Paul in his letter to the Ephesians was very clear on what behaviors need to be put off and put on to live in true holiness and righteousness. Verses in Ephesians specifically address:

Speaking truth (4:25)
Not letting the sun go down on your anger (4:26)
Not giving Satan an opportunity (4:27)
Not stealing, and performing good with your hands (4:28)
Speaking no unwholesome words, only those words which give
    grace (4:29)
Not grieving the Spirit with sin (4:30)

Putting away all bitterness, wrath, anger and clamor, slander and malice (4:31)
Being kind, tenderhearted, forgiving (4:32)

The demon-possessed may be violent. They recognize when they are dealing with Godly people. They can be rebuked and will leave as the name of Jesus is invoked.

Very specifically, a person does not move much beyond the Salvation Gate when he refuses to repent and make Christ-centered decisions and choices when the Holy Spirit prompts him to do so. The person willfully chooses to continue to maintain the "old mind" with its prejudices, hateful attitudes, seething anger, and bitterness. The person willfully chooses not to change anything about the way he *responds* to the world around him, and to the Spirit within.

A major component of repentance lies in recognizing that the "old ways" and "former habits" did not produce the joy and peace that come with Salvation. Millions of Christians today *want* to believe they can have joy and peace, and still live the way they once lived— complete with their pet sins and familiar bad habits and blatant greed. The truth is, fleshly living and spiritual growth are incompatible. One cannot keep one foot in the former life and another foot in the new life and walk with any degree of stability or balance, much less assurance and speed. It's impossible! Until a person *chooses* to change and repent of those things as the Holy Spirit convicts, the person will not move beyond mere Salvation.

And what about the person who says, "Salvation is enough"? I suspect the vast majority of Christians hold to the belief, "I'm saved. I'm okay. I'll be in heaven." Others hold a similar belief, "If I just get into heaven, that will be fine with me. I don't need to get overly good—just getting in is sufficient."

Any person who believes these limiting statements is a person who will not grow, and as a result will not experience the fullness of joy, the overflowing love of God at work in their lives, the maximum extent of "quality" or purpose to their lives, or receive the outpouring of God's rewards either here on this earth or in eternity. His witness for Christ will always be stunted by his failure to *choose* to change and grow. His effectiveness in ministry will always be thwarted. His inner satisfaction with life will always be at a lukewarm level.

Why Doesn't More Change Occur?

The reason lies in the exercise of our free will. The Holy Spirit does not move beyond the boundaries of our own free will. As long as we are trying to get "good" on our own, He does not act. As long as we place limits on what we allow Him to do, He does not act. When we express to the Lord that we are only willing to change to a certain degree and no further, He does not act.

When we don't see positive change in our lives, even with massive effort on our part, we tend to become discouraged. This is true in the natural and the spiritual. We begin to drift, with a "what's the use?" attitude.

What is it, then, that triggers a desire for change and growth and brings us through the next LifeGate?

In some people it is a growing dissatisfaction with the state of their lives. The way they are living is not bringing them the joy or peace that they deeply desire. They are bored with what is, and they have a gnawing feeling that God still has more for them to experience, to know, to say, to do, and to become.

For some people, this dissatisfaction with their lives comes about as they compare themselves to someone in whom they see much greater spiritual depth or a greater vibrancy of faith. They see in another person a more radiant spirituality or a more insatiable love for the Lord. They witness in another person's responses to life's circumstances a stability or confidence that they desire for themselves. They develop a desire for "something more" in their relationship with Christ.

The trigger is pulled when a person says, "I want ALL that You have for me, Lord. I am willing to live my life *your* way, and to do so in every area of my life."

This attitude describes "Yielding," the LifeGate that lies ahead.

The life-giving Spirit through Christ has freed us
from sin leading to death.
The life-giving Spirit controls our minds, giving life,
peace, and loving obedience to His known will.
Our spirits become alive and growing through
Christ living within us.
God is sharing His treasures with us.
Everything He gives His Son is ours as well.

Let us pray as Henry Nouwen once prayed:
Lord, I pray for the power of Your Spirit. Let Your power
invade me and transform me into a real disciple. Make
me willing to follow You even where I would rather not.
Amen.

ETERNITY

LifeGate 7: Sanctified Service

LifeGate 6: Anointing

LifeGate 5: Surrendering

LifeGate 4: Yielding

LifeGate 3: Converting

LifeGate 2: Seeking

LifeGate 1: Awakening

ASLEEP

Seven LifeGates:
The stairway to the transcendent life in the here and now.

chapter 6

Yielding

LifeGate 4

────────────────────

The second great question to ask yourself is this: *Are you willing to live on the divine level?* I encourage you to step back and see the process of transcendence as a whole.

- We must find the threshold of surrender.

- If we give up ourselves—yield—to the power of God ruling in us—unconditional submission and obedience—we will be clothed with power from the Divine.

- Self-surrender leads to the supernatural release of all our capacities. We become "sheer capacity" to the Lord because His power abides in us. Given our permission, He can do great things through us.

- We can use our gifts to God's highest purpose. We can be anointed or sanctified—set apart—for service. We can live our lives on a mission for God, in the here and now, and forever.

Is this process of transcendence something you are willing to embrace? If so, I have no doubt that God will do His work in you.

Yielding is the completion of the Conversion process. It leads to the joy, the fullness of life Jesus promised. It is the essential precondition to the Surrender LifeGate.

In Christianity we find a phrase common to most denominations: "Jesus is Savior and Lord." Indeed, He desires to be! In reality, most of us who claim to be Christians live in the understanding and assurance that Jesus is our Savior. We believe that he died a sacrificial and atoning death so that our sins might be forgiven and we might enter heaven after we die. It is with surrender that a person begins to understand and live in the fullness of the reality that Jesus is *Lord*. And Surrender lies *beyond* Conversion, and beyond the LifeGate of Yielding.

An important question each of us must ask ourselves often—ideally every day and in every important decision, choice, or crisis—is this: Is Jesus really the Lord of my life?

To honor Jesus as Lord means that He is allowed to set the agenda, determine the timetables, define the roles, signal the beginnings, mark the endings, require obedience, inspire emulation, and offer a fullness of character transformation. Jesus desires to be the *Lord* of those who claim He is Savior. He desires, by the power of His Spirit, to so infuse the believer with His own presence and power that the person gives up all claim to self and submits fully to His claim upon his or her life.

The LifeGate of Conversion, which moves us from Seeking to Salvation, is marked by belief. Nothing else must be done. It is faith alone—man's believing power—that moves a person to Conversion (Salvation). The necessary faith is already resident in man. Paul made this very clear when he wrote, "God has allotted to each a measure of faith" (Romans 12:3 NASB).

And what is it that a person is required to believe? Believing is focused on this truth about Jesus: The sacrifice that Jesus made on the cross was a complete, definitive sacrifice for the forgiveness of sin.

Yielding does *not* mean that the person loses his "identity." It means he takes on a new identity of Christ-follower! Neither does it mean that the person loses his "personality." It means that his personality is now cleansed and renewed and becomes more fully expressed. In yielding to Him, we become so intimately connected with God that He imparts to us His "forever" nature. Our future becomes unlimited, our potential boundless—not because of who we are or what we can do in ourselves, but because we are linked to the One who always is and the One who can do all things. Our finiteness is embedded in His infinite presence, wisdom, strength, and love. There is no more secure place to dwell than to be "in Christ" and to know that He has indwelled us by His Spirit.

Yielding fully to Jesus as Lord does not mean that the person loses her natural gifts or talents, nor does she lose her intelligence, emotional depth, or acquired skills. It means that natural gifts or talents are enhanced, intelligence and emotional depth are focused on new areas of understanding and wisdom, and acquired skills find new outlets for expression.

Conversion Compared to Yielding

We are converted or "saved" by the Holy Spirit, not by our own acts. We are acted upon. The Spirit converts, we do not. We are made "new creatures in Christ Jesus." We are birthed into the kingdom by the Spirit. We cannot make ourselves new; we cannot birth ourselves. Once we have been awakened and accepted Jesus as Savior, there is no going back to a Sleeping or Seeking stage. Our position in Christ is secured for us by the Holy Spirit the moment we first "believe and receive."

Conversion nearly always requires a convergence of three factors:

- Need: Awareness on the part of the person that he is separated from his Creator, cannot resolve all things by himself, and is sinful.

- Gospel: The Word takes on power as it is read and preached or proclaimed. It is inspired and changes us as we read it, allowing it to do its good work of encouragement or conviction.

- Spirit: The wooing and convicting power of the Holy Spirit both insists and persists in bringing a person to awareness that she must make a decision about Christ Jesus.

Jesus told us that we cannot be on the fence—we are either for Him or against. The Spirit draws us, ignites our faith to believe, and then seals our belief in God's eternal love. It takes all three factors to yield genuine conversion. Feelings of guilt do not result in genuine conversion. Head knowledge does not bring about salvation. Feeling conviction won't produce it.

A person who feels guilt for sin and separation from God, hears the message that Jesus is Savior, feels the Holy Spirit's convicting power inside him, and accepts and believes Jesus is his Savior . . . is saved.

Many who say they believe in Christ as Savior, I believe, are not born of the Spirit. Jesus was very clear that one must be born of water *and* the Spirit to enter the Kingdom of God (John 3:5). Unless the new birth is from God *through* the Spirit a person is not born again. Someone I know asked Peter Drucker, widely known as the father of modern management, if he was a Christian. His answer: "You are a better judge of that than me." He was a converted Jew and as he lay dying in a coma, those present heard him reciting the Lord's Prayer in German. His statement—*You are a better judge of that than me*—indicates that he wished for his very life to be an unmistakable witness.

Yielding is not a condition for admission to Heaven. All that is required is acceptance of Jesus Christ as one's Savior. Conversion is passive tense. In conversion, God takes the first step and we respond to Christ. Yielding is in present-active tense. In yielding, God holds out the fullness of life and says, "Claim it and it is yours." The choice to claim is ours. God wants not only our acceptance of Jesus as Savior, but our yielding to Him as *Lord*.

My son Tom's wife, JoKay, has two brothers, Jay and Jed. Jed was not a believer. Tom and JoKay prayed every day for Jed to yield. Then Tom was killed in a plane crash. JoKay continued her prayers for Jed's salvation. As their two children Kevin and Renee grew up, they joined the prayers for Jed. Kevin came to Jed's home in Southern California to read the Bible with him and to pray together. *This went on for forty-three years!* On March 15, 2009, Jed was baptized by Rick Warren. He joined the Saddleback Valley Community Church. In a sermon Rick had said, "Don't wait for a quiver in your liver, take a step in faith." This moved Jed to yield.

Is the fullness of life available to us the moment we receive Christ? Absolutely. But none of us fully avails ourselves of the availability! The process of receiving this fullness is one of yielding, moment by moment, step by step, day by day, to the leading, guiding, comforting, compelling, challenging, and ongoing voice of the Holy Spirit deep within our spirit.

Moving Toward Fullness

The Word of God speaks of a *fullness* of life repeatedly. Jesus said very clearly about His mission on this earth: "I have come that they may have life, and that they may have it more abundantly" (John 10:10 NKJV). Jesus taught: "If therefore your whole body is filled with light, with no dark part in it, it shall be wholly illumined, as when the lamp illumines you with its rays" (Luke 11:36 NAST). You have probably seen God's light in many people; they are aglow. A person's level of commitment, of belief, shows in the face of the believer. Some years ago I facilitated a strategic plan for Teen Mania, a youth ministry founded by the Reverend Ron Luce. They have a large campus in Garden Valley, Texas. There are one- and two-year character building programs with students living in campus dorms. They have "bowl" events, which draw thousands of teenagers. When I arrived, the students couldn't do enough for me. They took my bags to my on-campus room. They helped me at the cafeteria. They would sneak into the meeting room to look at my charts, which hung on the walls. They were "on the go with a glow." I have no doubt those kids left the campus and became "lanterns" in their own communities. The Spirit is like that.

Jesus was not speaking only of life in heaven, when he was talking about a full life. He was speaking of one's whole life here and now. He promises it will be radiant! To be radiant is to be joyous, happy, beaming, glowing—a point from which rays of light are emitted. To be radiantly alive unto God means:

- You are in possession of yourself—you know your unique gifts and talents.

- Your body is the temple of the Holy Spirit.

- You are on the path of a truly transformed life.

- You see and experience everything differently.

- Your values are changing.

- You are developing a close, personal relationship with God.

- You are in the process of becoming *fully* the person God created you to be for His divine purposes on this earth!

To possess yourself is to know who you are . . . a child of the Lord. The physical temple was the center of Jewish life. In John 2:19–21 (NASB) Jesus said, "Destroy this temple and in three days I will raise it up." The Jews, misunderstanding Him, said that the temple (Herod's) took forty-six years to build; how would He raise it up in three days? Verse 21 explains: "But He was speaking of the temple of His body . . ." Paul writes in 1 Corinthians 3:16 (NASB): "Do you not know that you are a temple of God and that the spirit of God dwells in you?" As a believer I see His hand everywhere: in the beauty of the sunrise and sunset, in the flower of a dandelion, in a baby's smile.

I see and experience everything and marvel at the delicate balance that makes earth habitable.

God's values are becoming my values. A close, personal relationship is developing with God because I am talking with Him. Sharing my joys, my concerns, my day. And, as with all loving fathers, He is speaking to me. I set aside time just to listen to Him. We cannot hear his voice if we are doing all the talking.

God makes a promise to those who love Him: "And we know that God causes all things to work together for good to those who love God, to those who are called according to His purpose" (Romans 8:28 NASB). Paul states our divine purpose in Ephesians 5:1, 2 (NASB): "Therefore be imitators of God, as beloved children; and walk in love, just as Christ also loved you." We are to glorify God in all that we think and do. First Corinthians 6:20 (NASB) instructs us: "For you have been bought with a price; therefore glorify God in your body."

In Conversion a person passes from death to life. The Holy Spirit comes to dwell within the person. He makes possible the works of transcendence—of turning all "old" things into all "new things" spiritually so that a person might truly reflect the life that Jesus lived. As described in chapter 5, this possibility lies in the exercise of the freedoms given by the Holy Spirit: the freedom to confess Christ, the freedom to repent, and the freedom to put off and put on newness of life—to adopt new behaviors and get rid of old ones. The *fullness* of a Spirit-led life in which a person thinks as Jesus thought, has the attitudes that Jesus had, displays the character and virtues that Jesus displayed, and speaks and acts as Jesus would speak and act, comes only with yielding fully to what the Holy Spirit prompts. In a manner not unlike our obeying traffic signs that say "yield," when we come to a decision or choice, we are challenged to "yield" to what the Spirit prompts, rather than to our inner urgings that tend to be swayed by boasting or jealousy or sinful cravings (1 John 2:16). The Spirit will nudge and keep nudging until you get it right and act in alignment with His will. The Spirit guided me to write this book. I was swayed away from it for a time by a famous pastor who overheard comments I was making about parenting. He interrupted, breaking into my conversation. "This is important, Tom. I will make my television facilities available to you and your colleagues at no cost and turn over the resulting product to you." Immediately I saw the potential of a parenting series on weekly television. We could visually demonstrate parenting as a Christian practice, dealing with individual situations. I wrote a forty-page outline and God said, "Enough for now. Not another word. Do what I told you to do next." I could not write one more word about parenting. When I went back to this book, a book on what amounts to a void in Christianity, Surrender, the words just flowed. All of my work life I have been seeing voids, and filling them. It's been my purpose.

Giving Him Your All

When a person accepts Christ as his Savior and is given the wondrous gift of the Holy Spirit, the Holy Spirit begins a *re-creating* process in that person's mind, emotions, and will. He brings healing to the two sides of the person's brain. The theoretical side of the brain is filled with wise advice. The person becomes "sound"—he is capable of doing what he thinks, and of thinking clearly about what he does. The Spirit makes whole what evil has corrupted. A person can intuitively and practically "think" as God desires and intends for a human being to think.

When a person has a fully sound brain, that child of God knows where he is going—really *knows*! Medical researchers are at the early stages of understanding the connection between sin and the brain. He is confident that all will end well. He has hope in the day in which he is living. He has joy in his heart. It is no accident that the final words used by the seventeen Old Testament prophets were focused on joy and hope! Their prophecies of God spoke to the inner reality that comes when we think as God desires for us to think, which leads to our acting in the way God desires for us to act. The end result is always a life of happiness and a delight in the future.

Can a person experience such happiness in the here and now?

Can a person have wisdom in daily life, regardless of circumstances, status, or experiences?

The answer to both questions is *yes*.

But such a person must yield his heart, soul, and mind to the Lord. He must submit all of his thinking, believing, and feeling to the refining and healing work of the Holy Spirit so that he can think, feel, and respond with wholeness.

Jesus said, "I want all of you. Your heart, mind, and soul." The heart is regarded as the seat of our emotions. Romans 10:10 (NASB) states, "For with the heart man believes, resulting in righteousness . . ." In Luke 10:25 (NASB) a lawyer asked Jesus, "Teacher, what shall I do to inherit eternal life?" Jesus asks him in the following verse, "What is written in the law? How does it read to you?" Luke 10:27 (NASB) gives us the lawyer's answer: "You shall love the Lord your God with all your heart, and with all your soul, and with all your strength, and with all your mind; and your neighbor as yourself." In Verse 28 Jesus responds, "You have answered correctly; do this and you will live." If we yield only our mind we have yielded only part of us. This is what I believe is the major void in the Church. We have to yield our emotions. To do this we must be emotionally ready.

Here is a construct that has helped many people:

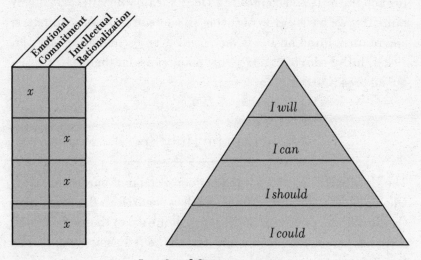

Levels of Commitments

The bottom three (*could, should, can*) are all intellectual rationalizations, not commitments. It is important to think things through. It's why we have minds. But "I will" is a real commitment. It is emotional. Use "I could, I should, and I can" statements to creatively consider what God might be asking you to do—but then move as quickly as possible to an "I will" statement if you wish to accomplish anything for the Kingdom. Only the committed accomplish anything. Millions of Christians lead a half life, never knowing the fullness of a life centered in Jesus because they are not fully committed believers, committed to following through on where the Spirit leads.

What I do know about yielding the will is that if a person chooses to take this step, the Holy Spirit is a ready ally. His comfort and presence are profound and often are manifested in very dramatic ways. We all know how Billy Graham's prayers were answered. Franklin didn't have a chance of going on, fighting God. God had a plan, a great purpose, for Franklin, just as He had for Paul . . . and Constantine . . . and Oswald Chambers . . . and you. The new normalcy to which God calls us is to *yield* to what *He* desires. If we are to discover our great purpose and His magnificent presence in our own lives, we must yield.

Through my yielding to God, I am enjoying a new career at the age of eighty-four; I'm passing on what I have learned through writing and training and counseling a legacy team who will carry on my ministry. We have a growing army of Paterson Process Facilitators; and in turn, I find my life is very exciting and stimulating—deeper, richer, fuller—during a phase that many consider themselves "used up" and ready to die.

Knowing the Holy Spirit

The Holy Spirit is the least understood Person of our Triune God. One night at a board meeting of my local church in Big Bear Lake, California, the president of the board admitted to those of us gathered that not only did he not understand the Holy Spirit, but that he found the concept scary. He told us that when he was a young man, his pastor spoke of the "Holy Ghost." He added, "And we all know ghosts are scary."

If we are to become best friends with God, and feel comfortable yielding to Him, we must come to know the Holy Spirit, appreciating His role through the ages and understanding rightly what it truly means to be "Spirit led." It simply is not possible to come into relationship with an *indivisible* Triune God and not know the *whole* of God. When the apostle Paul wrote about "knowing" in his letters to the early church, he was referring to direct experience. The knowledge to which he referred was not education—not knowing "about something" as one might know a philosophy. The knowledge was the result of *training,* knowing through application, practice, and experience.

Knowing requires personal relationship. Only then can any of us begin to comprehend the majesty of God's tri-part nature. Frankly, the best we can ever do in this regard is to "begin." No finite creature can ever begin to fathom fully the infinite Creator. *How do we get to know Him?* By reading and thinking on His Word. Daily devotions. Time set aside for God every day. Prayer . . . listening for His voice, being centered on Him. Many pastors who come to me admit that at home they do not have daily devotions, although they always enjoy participating while with me. Fortunately for us, our faith makes even the smallest degree of comprehension helpful.

When it comes to the Holy Spirit, the most important truth is this: He is the Spirit of Christ. Thus, to know Christ, we must come to know the Holy Spirit.

Jesus declared to His followers, including us: "I am the way, the truth, and the life; no one comes to the Father but through me" (John 14:6).

Jesus promised His followers, including us, "I will ask the Father, and He will give you another Helper, that He may be with you forever; I will not leave you as orphans, I will come to you" (John 14:16, 18).

Jesus foretold, "In that day you shall know that I am in My Father, and you in Me, and I in you" (John 14:20).

In John 14:17 the Greek word for "helper" (*paraclete*) encompasses rich concepts: advising, comforting, strengthening, encouraging, interceding, and exhorting. Jesus offered intercessory prayer (prayer for another) when on the cross he prayed: "Father, forgive them, for they do not know what they are doing" (Luke 23:34). As forgiven and freed people, the Spirit comes alongside to coach us, but He does so internally, at the very seat of our understanding and motivation, deep inside of us. Some Christians are graced with the gift of exhortation—encouragement. When they earnestly urge us to do something, it is powerful because the source of the strength is Divine (2 Corinthians 12:10).

While I believe that exhortation is a special grace, I also believe we should all be encouragers. We are all very good at tearing ourselves down; what we need is affirmation—affirmation of God in action. During the height of the Depression, I remember President Roosevelt's "Fireside Chats." Those were hard times, and we were desperate for any good word we could gain. In one radio address, the president said the famous words, "We have nothing to fear but fear itself." The words were powerful and timely—two adjectives that often accompany an exhorter's words to you.

In John 16, Jesus informed His disciples—both those who heard Him speak the words and us today—that the Holy Spirit, as the "Spirit of Truth" would guide Jesus' followers into all truth. It is the Spirit who searches all things and reveals what He has heard from Christ. He convinces the world of its sin and God's righteousness. He warns of coming judgment. He dwells in those who accept His Word. He enables those who accept His Word to fulfill what He has come to do in them and through them. When we accept His Word that He will fulfill what He has come to do in them and through them, and we know His purpose for us, we know . . . really know . . . that we cannot fail.

My pastor son, Tom, Jr., had been released from three churches by their senior pastor. He called me in tears. "What's wrong with me?" he cried. I went to him at once. As we circled the block where he lived, I put my arm around him and said, "Tom, there is nothing wrong with you or with your pastor, either. You are a young earthmover, an entrepreneur like me. These pastors think you want their jobs. They are insecure." (I've done LifePlans for several hundred pastors, and believe that pastors are the most insecure professional group I have ever worked with.) I spoke to some 750 pastors at a seminar at Rick Warren's Saddleback Church. Riding back to Ontario to get my car with a pastor and his wife, the wife said to me: "If you think our husbands are basket cases, talk to their wives."

Yielding to the Spirit is a Choice

Yielding to the Holy Spirit is a choice of our *free* will. It is an intentional, conscious decision we make. We have tremendous freedom in *choosing* to yield. When we do so, we embody the life of the Everyday Saint. Personally, I believe that God's intent is that all of His believers are to be saints. No paintings, statues, or veneration, just holy people who live to glorify the Lord in all that they do . . . as Paul said, "Living Sacrifices." And we get there by choosing to yield, again and again.

I was blessed to have such a saint for my wife. Ginny and I were married for most of my life when she passed away. She was born to be a nurse and served as an R.N. in a Catholic hospital where the nurses were taught the laying on of the hands—praying for patients while physically touching them. She loved children and simply could not walk past a baby. She helped patients to peacefully pass on to heaven, comforted their loved ones. As a five-year-old she would mix salt and water for her hypertensive grandma. "Here, I help you get well." Grandma would dutifully drink it.

God calls us to saintliness, but He does not force us toward saintliness. He calls and challenges, but He does not demand.

God created man and woman in His image, not as automatons or puppets. We are of unspeakable worth because He created us in His likeness. We have inherent dignity in that fact alone. "Let us make man in our image according to our likeness . . ." (Genesis 1:26).

He created us to be determiners, not to be determined. God created us to have compassion and the capacity to love one another. We are to be actively involved in God's ongoing creative, loving process on the earth—we are *co-workers with God* in this endeavor.

I have traveled the world. As a result, I have had the opportunity to witness personally how few people live in freedom. In much of the world women are chattels with few rights. In many nations a female receives little or no education. In some nations women are excluded from many religious ceremonies, including the most important ones. In some areas of the world, slavery is still practiced. In many of the most populous areas of the world, education is highly restricted and career paths are chosen for individuals apart from any consideration given to their personal desire or gifting. Countless parents, in nations such as China, have no freedom to bear more than one child. Freedoms related to expression of thought, political persuasion, free-market buying and selling of goods and services, and religious choice are strictly prohibited in almost half of the nations on earth. The democracy of the United States of America is viewed as dangerous and radical by more than half of the nations of the world.

Freedom is God's concept, not the plan of the first man, Adam. God's design for each one of us is for us to live unfettered in our human potential so we might become all we can become—to soar and to fly. To be free is to be truly alive. That is not to say that those who are free are not free of law. Rather, they are free to live within the laws of God's love, grace, and forgiveness. Adam did not live within God's laws or grace.

Hear the words of the apostle Paul: "Am I not free? Am I not an apostle? Have I not seen Jesus Christ, our Lord? Are not you my work in the Lord?" (1 Corinthians 9:1 NASB).

Not only are we given freedom to soar . . . but freedom to become servants. Paul, totally free, was nonetheless sent out by God to do the "work" of winning people to Christ and training them as disciples of the Lord.

Paul is our greatest role model of a God-transformed life. Three months before my wife Ginny or I knew she was ill—June, 1995—God interrupted my bedtime prayers and said to me, "Tom, you are to study the life of Paul." I didn't know Paul at the time; what I did know was wrong. I didn't like Paul; boastful, arrogant, know-it-all. How wrong can you be? Forgive me dear Lord. Eventually, I taught the Life of Paul to a small group class at my church. Here is the prayer I wrote for the class.

A Prayer for Our Life Being Lived to Your Glory

Father,

Your servant Paul led a life defined by a passion for Christ. His life was turned 180 degrees by Your love and his absolute surrender to Your will. He became a wholly new man.

Paul became Your servant and instrument of Divine Providence.

He lived Your Law of Love: He loved You with all his heart, with all his soul, and with all of his mind. You said that this is the first and greatest commandment. You said that another was equally important: Love your neighbor as yourself. He lived that part of Your Law of Love just as completely.

He rejoiced in You, our Lord, in all circumstances. He suffered just about every trial known to man, counting it as nothing for the privilege of being with You in glory.

You equipped him, comforted him, counseled him, and strengthened him. With You, Divine Savior, within him, he could not fail in the life mission You gave him. Together, You and Paul changed and are changing the world.

We want this for ourselves: Passion for You defining our lives, to be wholly new in You, to be Your instruments of providence, to love You with our all and others as ourselves, to suffer without complaint, rejoicing in the hope of eternal union with You, to be guided in all that we do by Your Spirit: Our mission, living out Your Master-thought for each of us.

May You be with each of us every moment as we study Paul's life. Guide our words, our thoughts, and our actions: may all be within Your will.

*May we grow spiritually, have our faith become a Paul-like faith,
overcoming whatever may happen to us. And, in and through You,
and Your timing, may we come into the freedom of absolute surrender
to Your will if that is not where we are in our walk at this time. May
our all be all to Your glory.*

Amen

Precious Freedoms for Our Choosing

Consider the precious freedoms described below—each of which God
offers to us through His grace as we choose His upward calling and
yield to the Holy Spirit.

- *We have the freedom to accept Christ's invitation to follow Him, or
to reject Christ and remain limited to our own self-reliance.* Jesus
is the sole path of life among the many primrose paths that
proclaim, "This way to the good life." Jesus meant what He
said: He is The Door. He is *the Way.* He is *the Truth.* No man
comes to the Father but by Him (see John 14:6). We have the
choice to take Jesus at His eternal Word or to deny Him. It is
the Holy Spirit who extends this invitation to accept Christ.

- *We have the freedom to be free of guilt through accepting what Jesus
did on our behalf in being crucified and resurrected, or to remain
in guilt and shame for sins that we intuitively know we have
committed.* Every person knows intuitively that he is either in
relationship with God, or is not in relationship with God. We
find relationship with Him through Christ.

Believing in what Jesus accomplished on the Cross on our behalf
moves a person from the shackles of guilt to the freedom of forgiveness. The cross is our means of becoming free of the shame warranted by our sin. Believing in what Jesus accomplished on the cross

is our means of receiving the gift of the Holy Spirit in our life. It is our means of being awarded the gift of eternal life. It is our means of experiencing an abundant life on this earth.

None of us can possibly love ourselves as much as God loves us. God is not the author of condemnation. Jesus clearly declared that He did not come to condemn the world, but that through Him the world might be saved (see John 3:17). God offers love, affirmation, and validation, forgiveness and restoration. Until a person accepts the fact that God loves him as much as He loves His only Son, Jesus—that God sent His Son so that we might be saved and restored—a person cannot fully accept himself. Until he accepts himself, he remains his own jailer. A tape will continually play in his heart, "Guilty as charged!" He will continue to be shackled by his own self-criticism, heaping condemnation upon himself. He will continue to seek out and pursue justification to give himself value that he believes he does not have—it's a vicious cycle. The only end to that cycle comes in saying, "I am a sinner in need of a Savior, and accept the truth that Jesus is my Savior."

It is the Holy Spirit who whispers in our hearts the hope of God's forgiveness and freedom of guilt as He woos us closer and closer to the cross. My son, Tom Jr., as he was drowning in a lake in Alaska, was heard shouting, "I am only a sinner saved by faith." He didn't need to pray that he would be saved: He was already saved.

· *We have the freedom to live the abundant fullness of life, or to live in true poverty of spirit.* True poverty is never finding God and therefore never finding one's self. True riches are gained when we empty ourselves of self and open ourselves to receiving the fullness of all God offers to us.

We have been fed a lie by the world—it is the lie that material wealth defines a person. Such a philosophy is the epitome of self-centeredness. It creates a poverty of spirit that results in a person being sick with a moral disease that is at the heart of all human conflict. We become possessed by our possessions when we trust our possessions to define us.

To a very great extent, social prestige or "status" is directly linked with our propensity for material wealth. The world holds out the belief that those who are powerful are equally rich, or have access to riches and to a lifestyle that is supported by wealth. Those who seek fame become slaves to fame; they crave it in increasing quantities until the craving consumes their souls.

When we empty ourselves of our own wants, however, and replace them with what God wants, we enjoy an abundance of those things that matter the most to us: love, fellowship with others, joy, peace, health, wholeness, and everything of lasting benefit. We are given a richness in the things money cannot buy and which no man can achieve on his own merit or through the blind adoration of others.

Ask any elderly or sick person what he or she most values and the person will probably answer: "Health, loving family members and friends, an inner peace, the ability to laugh, a feeling of purpose, meaningful work, a relationship with the Creator, and hope of life after death." These are not things that can ever be purchased off the shelf. They cannot be achieved by human effort alone. They are gifts from God, the Source of all that is good. They are gifts freely given in abundance to those who become Christ-centered.

"My grace is sufficient for you," is the answer Paul received after asking the Lord three times to take the thorn from his side. Sometimes it just takes faith to accept God's will—as it was for me to accept Debbie's passing. I believe this is why God allowed Debbie to speak to me. God works in an economy with no waste. There are no mistakes, so there is no waste. Ginny would wake up when ill with cancer and say, "Thank you, God, I'm alive."

It is the Holy Spirit who convicts us of these truths and gives us the courage to turn away from trusting wealth and fame, and trusting instead the bountiful provision and favor of God.

· *We have the freedom to learn, accept, and hide God's Word in our hearts, or to ignore it.* A person cannot find God or come to know Him in the abstract or through the words of learned men. A relationship with God is built through personal involvement with God—reading His Word, talking and listening to Him from the depths of one's spirit, and seeking to follow God's commands. A relationship with God comes as a person relies upon God's presence in every situation, every circumstance, every decision, and every challenge. Genuine freedom comes when we partake of God's Word as the manna of life—relying on it as food for one's spiritual growth and development.

It is the Holy Spirit who is the supreme Instructor of God's Word. The Holy Spirit is the protector of God's Word. Because of this our Bible has the Words of Jesus. Did you ever wonder how there was perfect recall of Jesus' words by His disciples? Jesus wrote nothing.

· *We have the freedom to develop a personal, intimate relationship with God, or to attempt to go it alone through life.* Being alone with God is never to be truly alone. When we are alone with God, we enter into an intimate relationship with Him that is beyond description. How can one really describe ecstasy, rapture? How can you fully describe love? It is a mystery. No one in heaven would want to return here. Being with God has to be a level of happiness that we cannot envision—but we can catch a glimpse of it here on earth. Pope John XXIII spent hours each day alone with God in meditation and prayer. My big objective now is to have the discipline to invest at least an hour every day alone with my Lord.

When the most important relationship in our life becomes our relationship with God, two things happen:

One, material things hold no fascination and we have no attachment to them.

Two, people are vastly important to us, but they do not dictate our actions. They are incapable of manipulating us spiritually or destroying us emotionally. We do not cling to others out of desperation to experience love. We have the unending, unconditional love of our heavenly Father. His love ultimately satisfies every human longing for love.

This is not to say that the surrendered person does not desire affection or expression of love from human beings. To the contrary! The surrendered person continues to have needs for affection, sexual expression, and loving friendships. The difference is this: the surrendered person does not base his worth or value on the degree to which others love him, approve of him, embrace him, or call him worthy. He draws upon the Lord alone for his definitions of worth and value. In return, the Lord gives the surrendered person a heart capable of loving others with an extraordinary amount of affection and pure love. Such a person is likely to experience a "receiving back" of love in amounts that are incalculable. What is given as an expression of love always comes back as a harvest of expressed love that is truly bountiful.

It is the Holy Spirit who awakens us to the tremendous power of God's love.

> • *We have the freedom to become all that we can become, and to rest continuously in the process of "becoming" throughout eternity or to close down and refuse growth, development, or the very concept of potential.* God desires to lead us into the fullness of the life He has willed for us. He wants to equip us to enjoy life and be successful in it. The life that He unfolds before us is never-ending; we will remain "under construction" all our days. In heaven we continue to become more like Jesus; we are constantly "becoming," in the present/active tense.

The more we grow and develop in our giftedness, the greater the opportunities God opens to us to use our gifts. If we don't know what our gifts are, we are not in possession of ourselves. We do not know who we are. If we do not know the gifts God has graced us with, we cannot know who we are in the deeper sense. When I studied the modern behaviorists as part of my MBA program, I had a life-changing "Aha!" I was later voted "most changed" person in my class, simply because I finally knew myself. (LifePlanning specifically addresses giftedness and will help you discover who you are. There are other tools but LifePlanning is a Spirit-led process for developing God's plan for your life in all of its domains: personal, family, vocation, Church/Kingdom, and community. To find out more about Life-Planning, see page 243) Perhaps you do not see yourself as gifted. If so, you are selling yourself short. Every one of God's children is given gifts. *No exceptions.*

The Bible speaks of God "enlarging our tents"—calling us always to greater application of our ministries by gaining in knowledge and wisdom in that He may be glorified. Our souls are priceless. Could we gain the world and lose our soul in the process? *Not* if we stay centered on God, becoming ever more close to Him. Jesus said, "Truly, truly I say to you, he who believes in Me, the works that I do shall he do also; and greater works than these shall he do; because I go to the Father" (John 14:12 NASB). The worldwide preaching of the Bible has greatly extended the Christian community. In Jesus' day, Christianity was a small sect, just one of many. To enlarge our tents we must be in greater possession of our souls. To whom much is given, much is expected . . . ever greater application of our ministries. Think about today's communications resources. As we rapidly become a digital world, there are tremendous opportunities for God's people to share God's Word and light to the world.

- *We have the freedom to accept the graces of God, or to reject them one by one.* When we become sensitive to the boundless ways in which God has and continues to care for us, we are humbled. We have the choice to either accept God's freely bestowed gifts, knowing that they are not awarded to us on our own merits, or to reject His gifts because we choose to "earn" gifts on our own.

God's gifts are given at His discretion. They are pure, eternal, and always for our highest good. Our highest good is to be in a deep, rich, full relationship with Christ, living a life defined by a passion for

106   DEEPER, RICHER, FULLER

our Lord; to live a righteous Holy life, to be His ministers, becoming masters of His gifts.

At times life is so hurtful that without God, life would not be worthwhile. When two of our four natural children passed on—Debbie and Tom, Jr.—I took Ginny and Tom's wife, JoKay, to Europe. Ginny broke down as we walked around the Arc de Triomphe in Paris. I was glad that she didn't live to see our son Jim killed years later. Paul tells us in Romans, "And we know that God causes all things to work together for good to those who love God, to those who are called according to His purpose" (Romans 8:28 NASB). I personally believe God causes all things to work together *to our highest good* if we love Him. All good fathers would have this intent. In my case, even after the death of some of my dearest loved ones, enough time has gone by that I can see how God is using me for His good purposes. It is no longer an arid faith that I am clinging to through the struggles of life, but rather a strong and growing faith that I am living.

Gifts we choose for ourselves can never be as beneficial as those God chooses to give us. No person can give himself another breath, another beat of the heart, another idea, another feeling, another inch of height, another opportunity, or another talent. All of life is a gift from God. When we deny ourselves of his gifts, we give ourselves disappointment and misery.

· *We have the freedom to spend eternity with God, walking in His paradise, or to choose a destiny apart from God, which is hell.* We are given the right of decision making: to experience a full life or a half life—to experience an abundant life, wholeness, or a diminishing life of fragmentation. Jesus said plainly that He came to offer us "life . . . and having it in abundance" (John 10:10).

John 1:4 presents one of the greatest concepts of Christianity: "In Him was life, and that life was the light of men." In John 14:6 Jesus is quoted as declaring that He is Life itself! In all, the Gospel of John presents the term "life" thirty-six times. Life refers to all that creates life, produces life, enables life, promotes life, enriches life, and gives meaning to life. It is the Holy Spirit who turns existence into exhilaration.

Many of those who take their own life have much of those things the world can offer: Comfort, ease, possessions. Yet they still commit suicide. The heir to the Armour meat packing fortune jumped out of a window to his death during the Great Depression. He was losing money at the rate of a million dollars a day. There were still millions to his name, but for him, life was hell. He was clinging to the things of this world rather than the One beyond, the One who promises the treasures of eternity—joy, peace, fulfillment.

The Invitation
Extended

The Holy Spirit *invites* us to allow Him to produce in us all that is good. Notice how an angel sent by the Lord approached Mary. He said, "Will you, Mary, consent to being the mother of the Messiah?" Mary's answer was simple, "Be it done to me according to Your Word." And with that yielding of her free will to the eternal will of God the Father, the Savior began to be formed in her womb as the shadow of the Holy Spirit overwhelmed her entire being.

The Holy Spirit's invitation to us is the same: "Will *you* consent to being the vessel in which I pour Myself and through whom I give Myself to the world around you?" Our challenge is to answer as Mary did: "Be it done to me according to Your Word." It is when we yield our free will to the eternal will of the Father that the Lord begins to do a work in us, and through us, that which is totally good, and that has the potential of lasting forever. There, in Bethlehem, more than two thousand years ago, the new humanity of Christ was born out of the old humanity of Adam. Here, in your own human flesh, God desires, by the power of His Spirit, to create a new humanity out of your old humanity.

The birth of Jesus changed the history of the world—His birth divided time into B.C. and A.D. God desires for *your* life, totally yielded to Him, to change the history of the world. Certainly the Lord does not call nor require you to do what Jesus did. His work on the cross was a one-time, definitive, substitutionary sacrifice for the forgiveness of sin.

Oswald Chambers wrote in *My Utmost for His Highest**: "The statement we so often hear, 'Make a decision for Jesus Christ,' places emphasis on something our Lord never trusted. He never asks us to decide for Him, but to yield to Him—something very different."

The Holy Spirit calls you to deeper and deeper intimacy with God the Son.

The Holy Spirit asks that you be willing to yield to Him the right to do the work that only He can do in you and through you.

The Holy Spirit calls you to be willing for Him to fashion you into the likeness of Christ Jesus.

If you are ready and willing to *yield*, the Holy Spirit will joyfully help you move through this LifeGate to the spiritual stage of Surrender.

---

* Oswald Chambers, *My Utmost for His Highest* (Grand Rapids, Mich.: Discovery House Publishers).

Not only does God give the choice to be free,
He provides the means to possess this miracle
of a life possessed by Him.
He fills us with His Spirit.
The Lord gives the tremendous privilege and honor of
living a life led by the Spirit,
moved this way and that by God,
protected from thoughts, deeds, and expressions that
are not within His will. Should we slip, He instantly
convicts, causing us to make amends.
We only need say yes to His provision.

ETERNITY

LifeGate 7: Sanctified Service

LifeGate 6: Anointing

LifeGate 5: Surrendering

LifeGate 4: Yielding

LifeGate 3: Converting

LifeGate 2: Seeking

LifeGate 1: Awakening

ASLEEP

Seven LifeGates:
The stairway to the transcendent life in the here and now.

chapter 7

The Call to Surrender

LifeGate 5

A s we pass through the LifeGate of Yielding, we find ourselves in a stage of spiritual transcendence described as Surrendering. God's ultimate grace is found at this stage.

In Conversion we accept Jesus and take hold of His hand.

In the Yielding stage we claim the fullness of a life in Christ. We yield to Him as our Lord.

In Surrendering, we deny self and choose to live the life He pours into us and through us. He takes full hold of us.

Without Surrendering none of us can do the "higher works" God has ordained for us.

I passed through this LifeGate of total yielding and entered into Surrendering in 1995. It happened in the aftermath of one of the most life-altering nights of my life. I arrived home one evening in late July and my wife, Ginny, asked me to call her physician. I replied, "Ginny, let me hear it from you."

We went out into our beautiful backyard forest-garden high in the mountains and sat down on a bench there. The evening shadows were beginning to envelop the grounds. The tops of our giant Ponderosa pines were aglow with the golden rays of the setting sun. The birds were gently singing their evening songs. In this splendor of nature, I was totally unprepared for the body blow that came as Ginny said, "I have lung cancer."

Everything deep within me screamed, "Oh no, God! Not my Ginny—the love of my life for more than fifty years of marriage—and with every passing year, a deeper, more tender love." My world was instantly turned upside down.

Surgery for Ginny was scheduled several weeks away. During the interim, I had an appointment with a client in London, England. As I pondered what to do, Ginny echoed the words that once had been spoken by our daughter Debbie decades before. Debbie had said to me, "Go, do your job!"

I knew I would be home well before Ginny's surgery, but I still would not have gone to England had she not insisted.

The first night in London, after having dinner with my client, I found myself in a hotel room all alone. With tears flowing down my cheeks, I fell to my knees in prayer, saying, "God, you have brought me to this point. I surrender. I give it all to You, whatever I am and all that I have. I will not attempt to make a deal for Ginny's life. There is no deal to be made. To try to make a deal would not only be wrong, but impossible. Whatever the outcome with Ginny, I give myself to You. Use me in any way You desire."

My prayer was not something I had preplanned. It was, however, very much a moment of Surrendering toward which the Holy Spirit had been moving me for a long time. I strongly felt impressed that God was going to give me a sign that He had heard my prayer.

He did.

For some time, I had known that I had a small skin cancer on my abdomen. For almost a year it had been ugly and bleeding but I had neglected to have it removed. That night, as I took my shower, the cancer dropped off, leaving a deep pit in my skin about a quarter inch in diameter. It bled profusely.

By morning, however, the wound had become only a pink spot, almost indiscernible. In my experience with other carcinomas in the past, I had found that it took about five months for a wound to reach that degree of healing. Yet in this case, a dramatic healing had occurred overnight. That was the sign I needed from God. I knew without a shadow of doubt I could trust God to heal my life, inside and out. I also felt a deep assurance that Ginny's life was in His hands.

When I was ready to trust God *fully*, something within me sloughed away just as that external skin cancer had.

Prior to that night, had anyone asked me if I was a surrendered Christian, I would have answered, "Yes, of course!" No doubt most believers would answer that same way. However, as I look back, I can see very clearly that until that night I had not truly surrendered *all* my life to Christ.

Surrendering requires great brokenness of heart. Surrender is made in weakness. Surrendering is made from a perspective of knowing that there is nothing you can do to control a situation . . . and that the *only* thing you can do is yield totally to the One who controls all situations.

In the wake of surrender comes peace, and as I look back, I also recognize that prior to that night I truly had never known God's peace.

A few weeks after this experience in London, a long-time friend said, "Tom, I've never known you to have such peace." He had no idea what had taken place in my life. He was simply observing my life and demeanor. I replied to him, "I have surrendered."

In true surrendering there is no going back. But it is progressive as we surrender even more of ourselves.

The Fullness of Yielding

One of the easiest and most thorough ways I know to describe surrendering is a "complete yielding." It is the fullness of "giving" oneself to Christ.

Through the years as I researched the subject of surrendering to Christ, I quickly discovered that there were very few writings about what it means to surrender fully to Christ—and how to surrender. Most of the writings were very old.

I reflected back over the sermons I had heard in churches I had attended for more than six decades. I could not recall a single sermon in which I was challenged to surrender my life *fully* to the Lord or about how I might truly follow God with my *entire* being. If such a sermon had been preached to my ears, I didn't hear it sufficiently to recognize its relevance to my life.

Certainly there may be churches in which surrender is a frequently addressed topic, but I had not attended any church—which included churches of several different Christian denominations that I had attended through the years—in which surrendering was advocated, nor had I received any instruction about how a person might go about "full surrender" to the Lord.

Perhaps the closest I came to an understanding about surrender was in reading books by Bishop Fulton J. Sheen. Sheen describes three levels of believers in his writings: those at the *moralistic* level with religious devotion; those at the *piety* level with an intense reverence for God, devoutly fulfilling their religious obligations; and those at the *mystical* level.

Sheen taught that the mystical level was the true "spiritual level," in which the soul was in direct union and communion with God through love, prayer, and contemplation. Regarding this third level, Sheen wrote, "Christianity . . . does not become so . . . until one enters the third stage: *The Mystical*. Here at last—where Christ *actually* dwells in our heart, and where there is an awareness rooted in love, and where the soul *feels* the tremendous impact of God working on itself—here is found the joy that surpasses all understanding."*

Prior to my full surrender to Christ I had been living at the moralistic level, and to some degree, the piety level. That night in London, the Lord took me to the other side of piety, to surrender that touched upon the mystical. It was the completion of a conversion process that had begun thirty years earlier. Far away from my home and my be-

---

* Fulton J. Sheen, *Peace of Soul* (New York: Whittlesey House, 1949), p. 269.

loved wife, I yielded myself to complete union with our Lord. I entered into a new fullness of life in Christ Jesus.

Once a person experiences this "fullness of life" that comes in the wake of a "completeness of yielding," there is no desire ever again to live in a lesser relationship with Christ Jesus.

Millions of Christians have settled for a type of "half life"—a moderate amount of avarice and a moderate amount of sin are allowed to coexist with godliness. Such people are like embryos too cool to incubate. They have just enough and no more—and those who are avid sports enthusiasts know that "just enough and no more" has never been a *game-winning* attitude. Such Christians continue to worry and have no real peace because genuine peace of soul comes only with total commitment. Peace comes when a person is totally freed from the bondage of sin, and that freedom requires a total yielding of self and a total renunciation of all sins that entrap and snare the human spirit. Not only is there no genuine peace, but there is little joy. The half life is a tepid life. Tepid water is not refreshing and it does not taste good. The same is true for a tepid spirituality—it does not give the refreshment of pure joy. Such joy comes with surrendering.

As is true at every stage of our spiritual transformation, God "calls" us to surrender. He calls to us as One who has already done the very thing He desires for us to emulate.

Few people seem to recognize this truth: *God obeys every law He demands of us. He fulfills every principle that He requires for us to believe.* Jesus said, "Whoever would to save his life will lose it; and whoever loses his life for my sake shall find it" (Matthew 16:25 NASB). Does God obey this law? Indeed!

Dr. E. Stanley Jones has written that he considers the verse below to be the most important verse in Scripture, or in literature anywhere:

> *For the Lamb in the center of the throne shall be their shepherd,*
> *and shall guide them to springs of the water of life; and God shall*
> *wipe away every tear from their eyes.*

(REVELATION 7:17 NASB)

This is such an unimaginable revelation that it could only come to us in the Book of Revelation. The principle is: "The Lamb (not a roaring lion, nor a mighty king of the hill, nor even a world dictator) is central to all things." The Word became flesh. To redeem us God sacrificed His Son: "He did not spare His own Son, but surrendered Him for us all; and with this gift how can he fail to lavish upon us all He has to give?" (Romans 8:32 NEB).

Dr. E. Stanley Jones has written: "Self surrender is at the very heart of God and is at the heart of all His attitudes and actions. When He asks us to surrender ourselves, He is asking us to fulfill the deepest thing in Himself and the deepest thing in us. It is not only the deepest in God—it is the highest in God."*

God calls us to Surrender, showing us in Jesus Christ what it means to Surrender. He calls us to Surrender knowing full well the price of surrender.

What Keeps Us from Full Surrender?

We don't have to look far—for many of us, no further than the nearest mirror—to see that we are not living out the great commandments of Jesus, nor are we living in the fullness of Jesus' promises of joy and peace. And the main reason is that we have not surrendered ourselves fully to the absolute authority of Christ over us.

There are a number of things that can keep us from yielding fully and thereby entering into a full state of "surrendering" to the Lord. Perhaps the foremost reason is that in order to give something, you must first possess it. To yield one's life to Christ *fully*, one must have a sense of possessing his or her life fully. Indeed, our *self* is what we give to God in surrender. If you are not in possession of yourself you cannot give yourself away to God, nor can you fully give yourself away to any person. If you are not in possession of yourself, you

---

* E. Stanley Jones, *Abundant Living* (New York: Abingdon-Cokesbury Press, 1942).

cannot fully give love to others, and certainly not unconditional love. You cannot fully trust others, including God, because you are not secure enough to do so.

Remember what it means to be "in possession of yourself." It means that you know who you are. You recognize your gifts—your natural talents and abilities, as well as your spiritual gifting that come as a result of God's grace and presence bestowed upon you.

I have a natural gift for design and strategy. I can see the whole. I am not mechanical in the least, and yet I received the basic patent for the ATM. I did not make a working drawing. Mine was a design patent. I visualized the personal identification number (PIN). The patent was assigned to my company, RCA. A strategic thinker can "connect the dots." I apply this gift in many ways. Strategic planning has been my professional life. God gifted me to teach. A client told me years ago that "There is a lot of teacher in you, Tom." I have been teaching ever since. I love it. This is both a natural and a spiritual gift that I incorporate in my work life as well as my personal life (see Romans 12:6–7).

The Master Potter broke the mold when He finished fashioning you—inside and out. To be in possession of yourself means that you know you have value to God as His beloved child, and therefore, you have the capacity to value yourself. The person in possession of himself knows, therefore, that he is a unique, valuable, gifted person.

Why is this important? Because if a person sees himself as totally without gifts, distinctive qualities, or value, that person will not believe he has anything to "offer" God. He will not see His life as a gift from God that he is, in turn, giving back to God. He will hold on to his life, striving to add meaning, value, and distinctiveness to his personhood.

Surrendering requires emotional and spiritual readiness to "give."

Another of my Christian heroes and life mentors, Thomas Merton, put it this way: "More precisely—we have to have enough mastery of ourselves to renounce our own will into the hands of Christ—so that He may conquer what we cannot reach by our own efforts."*

I referred earlier to Abraham Maslow's "Hierarchy of Human Need." His model looks like this:

Maslow's premise is that man cannot rise above the fulfillment of lower needs. For example, a person's primary needs are for sufficient air, water, food, sleep, and shelter. If a person is deprived of any of these basic all-consuming needs, little else will matter. He will spend his time and energy seeking to meet the basic physiological needs and will have virtually no perceived "need" for greater security, much less a need for recognition or self-actualization.

This is true on the individual level, and also on the community level.

Once the basic physiological needs are met, however, man will have a need for personal safety. Structures that were originally designed for shelter from natural elements of rain, wind, and cold will be "huddled together" as people seek to enhance their chances of security against both natural elements and war-seeking enemies.

Only after the first two levels are met can a person be concerned with receiving recognition for individual efforts. The one who re-

---

* Thomas Merton, *Thoughts in Solitude* (1958; repr., Boston: Shambhala Publications, 1993).

ceives recognition can then move on to the pinnacle of human need—the need to pursue one's potential and full reason for being. Self-actualization (or self-realization) is the full release of human potential.

Maslow contends, of course, that if a major emergency arises—such as a natural catastrophe, the threatening of one's home, or a major illness threatening one's life—the person can be reduced to meeting that level of need.

In today's world, with a massive number of white-collar executives still in the "permanently temporarily employed" category after corporate cutbacks and layoffs in recent decades, a large segment of a very talented population that was once at the self-actualization point has now been reduced to the level of seeking security. Those who remain behind in downsized companies also find themselves still struggling, in many sectors of the economy, at the recognition level. They, too, know what it once was like to live in the self-actualization zone. The result of being pushed down to a previously met level nearly always brings some degree of frustration, panic, fear, and depression.

This phenomenon is not only widespread among former white-collar executives, but also among formerly employed line supervisors and line workers in manufacturing sectors. Jobs that have migrated to other nations have left behind workers who were once higher on Maslow's hierarchy, and now find themselves scrambling for basic security.

Abraham Maslow, of course, did not deal with spiritual transformation. His model is strictly psychological-sociological. As Christians our concern must be for the *whole person,* including the spiritual. One of the simplest ways to understand spiritual "readiness" for surrender, from my perspective, is to regard spiritual transformation as the ultimate extension of self-actualization.

In yielding self—in essence, giving up self—one finds self. That is a great mystery of the Gospel, but nonetheless true. To be *fully* actualized, a person must be *fully* transformed.

A person who is struggling to meet physiological needs and the need for physical security will find it very difficult to deal with a spiritual void in her life. As the old adage goes: "A person cannot hear the gospel on an empty stomach." To a great extent that is true. The first missionaries to China fed the Chinese rice. They were hungry. It's hard to hear God when you hunger. Jokes were made about "rice Christians" when I was a boy. I thought feeding them rice made great, practical sense.

Our instinct is for survival. It isn't a conscious thought but an instinct. If we are threatened with imminent death, we are going to be most concerned with removing that threat. Seeking God begins when we have secured our basic needs for the maintenance of human life.

Conversion may very well flow out of a deeper awareness of our need for *inner* security. Even after external security is achieved, one has a need for emotional and spiritual security. Nothing has ever hurt me as much as Debbie's death. But it is an example of how God brings forth good from our suffering (see Romans 8:28). The person still carries sin's weight of guilt, which bears a threat of its own on the soul. The ultimate inner security is found only in Christ.

Surrendering requires a degree of emotional maturity and well-being. It comes when a person discovers that the praise and accolades of the world will never be able to supply what a relationship with God can. In order to come to that point, a person must be in relationship with others and have received a degree of recognition and approval. It is only then that a person is capable of fully recognizing that human relationships and recognition cannot fully satisfy the longings of the heart.

A person who is struggling to become emotionally whole in the wake of abusive or damaging relationships and experiences—a person who has suffered as a victim—is a person who has never known deep positive recognition and approval. As a result, that person is woefully lacking in self-worth, or an ability to "esteem" their own unique creation. Such a person is likely to find it very difficult to surrender their life to God. He is still in a struggle to feel as if he has a life worth surrendering! Too much risk is associated with surrender for the person—indeed, the very concept of surrendering has been tainted by feelings of loss, vulnerability, pain, and violation that have come as a result of *forced* submission at the hands of an abuser. For a person to be able to surrender his life to the Lord, that person must first be healed—at least to a significant degree of wholeness—from the wounds of abuse. Surrendering is a *voluntary* process in all respects, and as such, it represents a tremendous step forward in freedom for the abused person. Before a voluntary step can be taken, however, an abused person must come to grips with the past *forcing* of submission and recognize fully that Christ does not force a person to surrender, but rather, invites a person to surrender as an act of release and freedom, not as an act of denigration, defamation, or degradation.

With a strong perception of approval and recognition in relationship with other human beings, a person can become emotionally mature. Emotional maturity is a requisite for full surrender.

Emotional maturity, of course, is not linked to chronological age. Many people remain emotionally immature for decades. Others come to maturity very early in life. Generally, those who are emotionally mature early in life enjoyed childhoods in which they received tremendous amounts of unconditional love, full approval and support of their parents, and positive recognition from other adults in their world—perhaps teachers, pastors, or adults in other leadership roles. An emotionally mature person is a developed adult whose emotions are compatible with their physical adulthood.

If you have not yet come to the point of full surrender in your life, it may be that you still have some "recognition needs" that you need to face. You may have some inner emotional work to do prior to your being prepared for the next step. I received great help from a Christian psychologist. On our first session he observed: "You are filled with tension." I denied this. He said: "Look at your hands." I was sitting in an overstuffed chair and clutching both arms of the chair . . . totally unaware of what I was doing.

What might a counselor say to you? About your emotional, mental, and relational health? Your progress as a maturing adult? As long as we have unmet physiological, security, and recognition needs we cannot surrender fully. We are locked into a quest for self-preservation and self-identity. We feel we must defend, care for, and protect ourselves. Total surrender to God strikes at the foundation of our physical humanity—the instinct of survival.

We are *ready* to yield and to enter a state of full surrender when we acknowledge we cannot be our own defense, provide for ourselves, or be our own safety. As God's Word says, "The eternal God is your refuge, and underneath are the everlasting arms; He will thrust out the enemy from before you, and will say, 'Destroy!' " (Deuteronomy 33:27 NKJV).

The Blockage of Self-Centeredness

A second major factor that keeps us from yielding fully and entering into full surrender is pride. Augustine confessed, "I want to be good but later, not now." Many "saved" believers in Christ hold a similar viewpoint! They want to have their own way before they are willing to allow God to have His way.

My son Jim went through a very serious, life-threatening experience. His strength was gone. He had no vitality to his steps and life became a very painful, depressive existence for him. Following a thorough physical examination, followed by further medical tests, physicians concluded that the problem was a blockage in the arteries leading from his heart. Angioplasty was performed and the blockage removed. Overnight, my son felt like a new man.

Oh, that all of life's "blockages" were so readily diagnosed and cured!

Through my years of working with people in various industries and at all "stages" of life, I have come to a conclusion: Virtually all of the *relational* problems we experience are rooted in self-centeredness—including problems between husbands and wives, parents and children, neighbor and neighbor, employers and employees, producers and consumers, elected officials and those who put them into office, and so forth. Problems on the international scene often can be boiled down to relational problems rooted in the self-centeredness of neighboring tribes, cultures, or "people groups."

The good news that Christ holds out to us is surrender. Surrendering causes a *positive* pattern to be created. When a person surrenders to Christ, his life becomes Christ-centered as opposed to self-centered. Individuals who are Christ-centered produce families that are Christ-centered, and they, in turn, create communities and eventually nations that are Christ-centered. When a person, family, community, or nation yields to what *Christ* desires, a flow of forgiveness, reconciliation, restoration, healing, wholeness, and generous service to others is put into effect. The end result is not only coexistence but genuine peace—and out of peace, opportunities for genuine prosperity, alliances that produce genuine protection, and harmony that produces genuine loving relationships. There is no problem on earth that cannot be solved when Christ is put at the center of the problem-solving process!

The Detours of the Enemy

Yet a third factor that can keep us from a full yielding of self is that the enemy of our souls tempts us continually to take detours, to give in to self-centered desires and goals, and to ignore the leading of the Holy Spirit as He seeks to direct us and guide us into the paths that are the most productive and fulfilling for us. Any time we yield to the devil's temptations, we are *not* yielding to the Spirit's guidance. Our yielding is misplaced.

Although we often do not recognize them as such, times of suffering are nearly always filled with temptation. Certainly when we are in great pain, grief, or agony the temptation is strong to ask, "Where is God? Where is my deliverance? Where is my help?" When suffering comes, our first response is often one of withdrawal into self, rather than an outpouring of ourselves to God. Like a wounded animal running to seek refuge in a cave, we pull away from God and others to nurse our wounds, regain our personal strength, and refocus our perspective.

In reality, suffering is a tremendous factor that is often used by God to draw us into surrender. Suffering does *not* need to be a temptation to turn away from God. It *can* be a catalyst for spiritual growth. In our emptiness and loss, there is suddenly room for God to move in big ways. About a year after Ginny passed, I began to pray for a wife. Paterson men have to have someone to "do for," someone to love. A friend told me about a neighbor who had lost her husband and moved to the San Francisco Bay area. The friend thought this woman might be interested in having me do a LifePlan for her son, Eddie. Some weeks went by, and there was no call. I asked for her number so I might call, and after the friend asked Meryl if it was all right, I received her number.

I called Meryl and we struck up a friendship over the phone. Each morning, I'd begin my day by calling her. Two weeks went by and at three in the morning, God awakened me and said, "I have selected Meryl for you and when you propose, she will accept." Mind you, we had never even met! We'd not even seen a picture of one another.

But Meryl called me three hours later, and when I heard her voice, I got down on my knees and proposed. She accepted, as God had promised. Now at our age, long engagements are not advisable, but she was on her way to Europe with her niece. Every night I called her, at about her bedtime, while she was traveling. When she returned, I was waiting for her. As her plane landed, I said to God, "You have selected her for me. I don't care if she's good looking or ugly, fat or skinny. I am marrying her."

Two weeks later we were married and we had six very good years together. She was a wonderful Christian lady, with a great sense of humor and wonderful skill as an artist. She used to visit nursing homes and ask who never received visitors, and then went to those people to spend time with them. I am grateful for the life we shared and the time we had, but Alzheimer's slowly pulled her from my arms. When I had a stroke, and could no longer care for her, her son came from Phoenix and took his mother home with him. I never saw her again. Meryl passed away a year later.

I have studied the lives of a number of saints through the ages. It seems to me that virtually all of them experienced a season of suffering. In most cases, suffering appears to have "informed" these saints that they could *not* defend themselves successfully at all times, were not self-sufficient, and could not succeed in their own power. In spite of their best efforts, they failed. In spite of their best plans and schemes, they experienced hardship, uncertainty, and pain. Suffering confirmed to them that they were finite creatures living in a fallen world. Suffering was a stark reminder that human beings sin and are surrounded by others who sin. Suffering was a mirror that reflected the truth that no person can see all, know all, or be all in all. We do not rule the world—in truth, we cannot rule our own selves every moment of every day. We cannot *help* but suffer.

The apostle Paul described the conflict each of us experiences. He wrote, "But I see another law in my members, warring against the law of my mind, and bringing me into captivity to the law of sin which is in my members. O wretched man that I am!" (Romans 7:23–24 NKJV). Paul then asked, "Who will deliver me from this body of death?" From within his being came the answer: "I thank God—through Jesus Christ our Lord!" (Romans 7:25 NKJV).

Suffering *can* bring us to the point where we now with clarity see that we cannot resolve our own anxiety, deliver ourselves from our own stress, or manufacture peace for our souls. Such a realization can bring us to a full yielding of self. As is the case repeatedly in our spiritual transformation, we can *choose* to draw these positive conclusions that move us forward in our spiritual transformation—or we can *choose* to give in to the enemy's temptation in the face of suffering, "curse God and die" (see Job 2:9).

A Decision Made with Faith

In the end, a full yielding—a full surrender—is a decision made with faith. And the very good news is that every person has been given a measure of faith. Every person *can* believe. There is an expectancy and a knowing that accompany believing. Faith becomes fully effective when we believe with great *conviction* that God will hear our heart's cry and will respond out of the infinite love, goodness, and greatness of His own nature.

Some time ago, a man came to me for a LifePlan—a process I describe in greater detail later in this book. We had spent a full day together gaining a good understanding of his gifts and the ways in which God had molded him through life-changing experiences. We had discussed the need for surrender and he had acknowledged that he desired to surrender and had not yet surrendered his life to the Lord. On the second morning of our time together, he joined my wife and me for a time of prayer and reflection in the sunroom of our home. As we prayed, this young man voiced to God, "I want to surrender to You but I am afraid. Help me."

We left the sunroom and moved to my office to begin the second stage of the LifePlan process, and I couldn't help but notice a profound change in his face and demeanor. He suddenly was more relaxed, more vulnerable, more expressive, more radiant. I said, "You surrendered, didn't you?"

He nodded. In merely admitting to the Lord that He *wanted* to surrender, he had given voice to his own faith that he *could* trust God in this matter. God accepted him where he was, and indeed had helped him to yield fully.

In the same way we come to Christ in faith initially, we move by faith into every stage leading to full surrender. While asking for God's help, we must be willing to take an *active step* toward making Jesus the Lord of all we are and have. And though, at times, we may feel distant from God or we may struggle with various issues associated with our faith, we must believe with all our heart that we are becoming more and more like Christ, and are more and more surrendered as we take active steps toward yielding more of our lives to Him.

Nothing Withheld

I have facilitated LifePlans for hundreds of people who profess a relationship with Christ. Yet, almost without exception, during the course of the two days we spend together, they admit that there is something in their life that they are withholding from God. There seems to be an area in each person's life that he clings to, not wanting to turn that area over to God. In many cases, it is a person's career or material possessions. Or, it may have been something from their past—a hurt, problem, or shameful experience that they continue to cultivate and hold on to emotionally and mentally, perhaps fearing the judgment of God, or perhaps fearing that God will *not* act to bring judgment on the person who has inflicted the pain, caused the problem, or initiated the shameful experience.

On one occasion a person very bluntly confessed, "I'll surrender my life to God when I retire." This man had a high income and an important position in his firm, and he wasn't prepared to abandon it. He felt certain that if he surrendered his life fully to Christ, he would need to abandon his business, his income would drop dramatically, and he would be found "in want." To him, surrender meant "to lose."

I can relate fully to that viewpoint. I once held to a similar opinion.

Bob Buford is a great Christian entrepreneur. He is the author of two outstanding books, *Halftime* and *Game Plan*. He also has a daily prayer list of ten people, including me. I count Bob as one of my dearest friends.

A number of years ago Bob told me that he was praying for me to give myself to Kingdom services. The services that can be of optimum support are those emanating from our gifts. I responded, "I'll give my life fully to God when I can afford it." His response was immediate and intense. He called upon the "Hound of Heaven" to chase me, and for there to be no escape. Bob also said, "If you don't want to multiply, Tom, don't come around me!" To multiply is to add to Kingdom growth. Bob will put "100X" on his gravestone. Needless to say, I did want to multiply and I did want to maintain my deep friendship with Bob.

Looking back, I see how foolish my statement was. Since I have fully surrendered my life to Christ, I have experienced no loss of income. And I have experienced the greatest sense of fulfillment and purpose I can ever imagine experiencing.

Many people assume that when they surrender their lives to Christ, they will be required to pay a price or to give up something. For some, this means giving up a good pagan life, complete with all of the "sinful pleasures" they have grown to love. For others, it means giving up a pleasant, moralistic, and casual Christian life with few constraints on one's time, giving, or activities. A wealthy man once came to me for counsel. He thought surrender would entail giving up his six-thousand-square-foot home. I reminded him that God only wants us to surrender what should not be in our life: jealousy, deceit, selfishness, judgment, anger, grudges, hatred, prejudices— whatever is keeping us from God. I said, "If your home is keeping you from God, that is a serious concern you need to address. Otherwise, why would God want to keep you from your home? In all likelihood, He desires for you to *use* your home for ministry purposes that you have not yet considered."

The decision to surrender fully comes down to a matter of trust. Many do not want to put their total trust in the Lord because they are not certain that the Lord is totally trustworthy. As a support for their lack of belief, they point to the evil that exists in the world—such things as abject poverty and hunger, abuse of innocent children, virulent diseases, and so forth.

The truth of God's Word is that we live in a fallen world and we have continued to choose evil over good for millennia. God has given us the privilege of choosing . . . and we have made very bad choices as the human race.

If God were a dictator He might abolish evil in the blink of an eye. But He does not act as a dictator because to do so would destroy the human freedom of choice. Through the millennia we have created for mankind an environment in which poverty, hunger, abuse, and disease continue to exist. When we stare into the face of God and demand, "Why don't You do something?" I have no doubt that the Lord speaks back to us as the collective human race: "Why don't *you* do something?" God's definitions for good and evil are clear, and as Creator, He holds all the options for defining what is good and evil. God's choice is always for good. Ours is not.

Even at what the Bible describes as the end of the age—a terrible and awesome Day of the Lord—there is no representation that God is ready or happy to destroy human beings. His desire remains that we human beings might choose good, and choose Jesus the Son.

Those who choose evil . . . become evil. They become in bondage to sin. They cannot free themselves from it.

Those who choose good . . . become good. The catch is this—the first and foundational choice that we are capable of making for good is to say, "I choose Jesus. I choose to believe in Him. I choose to accept and receive Him as my Savior."

All other choices for good must flow from that first and primal choice. It is only as we make that choice that we receive the Holy Spirit's empowerment within us to turn away from evil and make subsequent "good choices."

I am speaking now, of course, of choices that are genuinely good—from God's perspective. Mankind can and does make routine choices for "good" that are according to man's definitions of what is good. It is good to drive within the speed limit, drink pure water and breathe pure air, attend church, stay employed, pay taxes, and so forth. Within the definitions of mankind's "good," a person might make "good choices"—and even in so doing, completely miss the only truly good choice that is required of man.

Again, it is God the Creator who does the defining for His creation. Jesus said, "Only the Father is good." Only the Father is motivated continually to love and to exhibit not only good character but to impart good character through His Spirit. Only the Father is motivated continually to extend mercy and forgiveness and to manifest miracles that are for a person's eternal good.

The choice we must make is for good according to *God's* standards and definitions of what is good. And that first "good choice" we make is a choice to receive Jesus as Savior.

One of the apostle Paul's central doctrinal themes in the New Testament writings is that God is righteous, perfect, and through His grace we are forgiven. As a recipient of His grace, the surrendered soul wants to live in a manner consistent with His righteousness. The surrendered person has a *desire* to choose good, to think "good," to speak "good," and to do "good."

It is the Holy Spirit who guides or counsels us into making good choices—and right decisions. Paul wrote to the believers in Rome: "You are controlled by the Spirit if you have the Spirit of God living in you." He then added, "And remember that those who do not have the Spirit of Christ living in them are not Christians at all" (Romans 8:9 NAST). It is the Spirit who enables a person to reject decisions and actions and temptations to do those things that contribute to death, and to pursue the decisions and actions and desires to do those things that promote life, both an abundance of life now and eternal life in the future.

Extraordinary and Eternal

We do the ordinary. God does the extraordinary. Not only does He work in us, but through us and all around us. Other people respond to the mission the Spirit anoints us to accomplish. The surrendered person does not need to *demand* allegiance or obedience. God moves on the hearts of others even as He moves on our hearts.

The psalmist wrote, "You will show me the path of life; In Your presence is fullness of joy; At Your right hand are pleasures forever" (Psalm 16:11). He was speaking of God's eternal life for the believer.

The process of transformation and transcendence is never complete. It continues throughout eternity. How exciting it is to think that we can continue to grow in faith and in our responses to life—and as we do, experience living on the Divine level! We become, more and more, like Jesus Christ in our character and nature. What a possibility! How wonderful it will be to one day be able to think, feel, and respond as Christ did and does.

I truly do not know anything more exhilarating than to live a surrendered life of anointed and loving service. This IS the life we were meant to live!

If God is everything we center upon, we are a Christ-centered soul.
If we are Christ-centered, we are happy, radiating sunshine to
all around us, lightening their day, giving energy, lifting
their spirits—we are a source of life.
The Christ-centered soul is moved by the Spirit in revelation,
moment-by-moment living in and through Christ.
The "I will" Christian lives by the manifold gifts and graces of God,
on a spiritual level with one foot in Heaven and the other on earth.
The Spirit comforts, guides, encourages, nudges, and
takes the surrendered soul beyond his best,
to what God has in mind.
Faith gives the courage to move in the way that truth demands.
The wisdom of the Christ-centered soul transcends all other
learning from books or personal experience, for it is the wisdom of
Christ-in-me. It is the wisdom of the Supernatural.

chapter 8

The Surrendered Life

A *friend of mine, who has* lived a surrendered life for a number of years now, recently told me about a woman named Sandi. I suspect that Sandi's background is similar to that of tens of thousands of people, if not more.

Sandi grew up in a very traditional Christian denomination. She was baptized as an infant and grew up believing that she was a Christian on the basis of that event, which occurred when she was ten weeks old. Her family went to church occasionally—usually "in the wake of a crisis" as Sandi recalls, but they never missed a Christmas Eve or Easter service. When Sandi was twelve, she was enrolled in a class that she attended regularly for several months—the class was designed to teach her the catechism of the church and to prepare her for a singular event of "confirmation" in which she was called upon to affirm for herself what her parents had affirmed for her at her baptism—that she, indeed, believed Jesus is the Christ.

If you had asked Sandi at any time during the first thirteen years of her life if she was a Christian, she undoubtedly would have said yes.

Then at age fifteen, Sandi went on a youth retreat during which Jesus and His sacrificial death on the cross was explained to her in a way she had never heard it explained before. She prayed with a counselor during a prayer service at the retreat to open her heart to Jesus and accept Him as her Savior. She told my friend, "I had such wonderful feelings in that hour—such feelings of being forgiven and loved and clean from the inside out." As the months passed, Sandi fell back into the regular patterns of her life, which included very little church attendance and virtually no prayer or reading of Scripture, and over time, she began to wonder if the wonderful feelings of the youth retreat were related to something, in her terms, "teenagerish." If anybody had asked Sandi, however, if she was a Christian, she would have said yes. And if they pressed the point as to whether she believed Jesus was her Savior, she also would have said yes. Sandi went to college, and occasionally attended a college group that discussed faith issues. She earned a master's degree, married, had two daughters, divorced, remarried, divorced, grieved greatly after the death of her father, and changed jobs three times—and all of these major life events involved a nominal church attendance. She had her daughters baptized, sporadically attended church, but as in her childhood, never missed a Christmas Eve or Easter service.

Then the time came—nearly twenty-eight years later when she was in early forties—that she became friends with two women who seemed to have a depth to their faith that she had never encountered before. They knew their Bibles in a way that Sandi didn't know was possible. They prayed as if they actually had a living and breathing relationship with the Lord. They talked openly about Jesus, again in her terms, "as if He lived in their homes." Sandi went on a prayer retreat with those two women and came home a changed woman. She phoned a friend and announced with great enthusiasm, "I made my surrender! I made my surrender!" The Holy Spirit used these two prayer warriors to make the moment when the Spirit moved Sandi to surrender. While the three were in prayer Sandi felt the presence of the Spirit as never before. She felt clean, lighter, and with peace of soul. She knew she had yielded her spirit to the Spirit of God.

Indeed, that is precisely what had happened. Sandi had put her *full* trust in Christ Jesus and surrendered her *full* life to Him, believing that He would lead her into everything He desired for her to experience, protect her from all evil, and "walk and talk" with her through every event of her life. She said to our friend several months later, "Everything in my life is based upon Jesus. *He's* the focus. He's the ultimate bottom line."

Living "New"

It is at the point of fully Yielding that a person makes a complete renunciation of confidence in self and claims a total reliance on the presence and power of God. A practice of Christ-like behavior, attitudes, and responses becomes paramount. The person has a passion to walk with Christ and to become Christ-centered.

It is in the phase of Surrender that a person experiences the "beginning of the end" of the battle between the carnal and spiritual. In military terms, the "beach is secured." There is usually a fuller revelation of God's purpose for the surrendered believer.

But understand that not all things will be immediately clear. In reality, surrender is a *process* wherein God will show a person only what He knows that person can handle. This requires patience on the part of the surrendered person, as well as on the part of others (surrendered or not) who may live with or be in close contact with the person. We are a nation of people who like to get quickly to the "bottom line." But, surprise! There is no bottom line, nor will there be a bottom line to surrender until we meet our Lord face-to-face. We are in a race that has no finish line this side of eternity. In fact, I believe there is no finish line even in eternity. I find that exciting!

Surrender is not a one-stop moment. For many people surrender is a glorious moment in their lives. For others it has been a progressive aspect of their life. They are surrendered but cannot point to a particular moment. It is the result of yielding one part of our life at a time. Our failures, our past, our successes, our present, the future.

We wake up one morning and find that we have placed our full life in His arms.

I have personally witnessed many surrender moments when a person's life has radically and forever changed. Often the Spirit gives indication of His presence. I'll give you one example. A senior executive of a manufacturing company came to me for a LifePlan. His inner turmoil was such that I knew this man had not fully yielded. He was at a career crossroads. "You have not surrendered to God," I said.

"No, I haven't," he returned. "I am an unsurrendered believer."

"Your numbers are legion," I replied. We agreed to pray for his surrender that night. (I do not bring up the subject of total yielding unless the Spirit guides my tongue to do so.) The next morning he told me that he got up early and walked all the way up the hill of our street and stood at the end of the blacktop road for a minute. Then he started to turn to go back down. The Spirit said to him, "Not yet." Then the Spirit said, "Step off into the dirt." It was muddy but he did as instructed. Next the Spirit said, "Now turn and go down the hill." All the way home he heard the Spirit say, "Accepted, accepted . . . accepted." Why this sequence? I believe he was being taught obedience to God's will before his surrender was completed. He is living the life of a new person, is now heading his own company, and is experiencing peace of soul as well as greater success in his vocation.

Up to this point of surrender in the faith journey, a person may periodically have a feeling of Christ living within. There may be a few nominal changes of behavior, but rarely are the changes permanent. It is not until *after* an experience of surrender that the surrendered person lives in a fuller understanding of "Christ in me."

Let me share with you two factors related to this process of seeking and "seeing" the potential for a Godly life.

First, the surrendered person is increasingly aware that while he "lives" *in* this world, his identity, values, and purpose are not *of* this world. He knows that his highest purpose is to express his identities, values, and purpose, and in so doing, to have an impact on others around him. He has an understanding about what he must do, what he must become, and why he is on earth. There is a growing urgency to be about things that are eternal, not temporal. He understands with greater depth the words of Jesus: "We must work the works of Him who sent Me as long as it is day; night is coming when no man can work" (John 9:4 NASB).

I'll use myself as an example. My identity is with the Christian Community. I marvel that I live in two worlds at once: God's Kingdom and this world; two communities. My values are to be a shining light, radiate love and be an example of the Christian life; to be moral and just to all and be a servant-leader. My purpose is to put the gifts He entrusted me with to His glory and highest purpose. I do not hesitate to say grace when dining in public; in fact, I cannot begin to eat without joining hands and thanking God for His provision. If this sounds just too Goody Two-shoes to you I will tell you that many people have stopped at our table to say, "Thank you, it was good to see this."

Second, the surrendered person is increasingly aware that the Holy Spirit is the one who "reveals" purpose, just as surely as the Spirit imparts breath to the body. It is the Spirit who enables a person to "find" those things that give life its ultimate sense of purpose and fulfillment. No person can truly discover the depths and heights of her own creation—her gifts, her calling, her desires, her uniqueness as a human being—unless the Spirit enables that process. In other words, we cannot "know" ourselves fully apart from the Spirit revealing to us who we are in Christ Jesus. *It is the Spirit who perfects the believer as the believer continues to yield to His perfecting work.*

The LifePlanning Process is a Spirit-led process. I have said that I would never dare to speak as boldly as I do if the Spirit were not a full partner in the process. Our LifePlan facilitators depend on the Spirit as I do. Consultants try to "crack the case" as soon as they can. LifePlanning is not consulting. It is ministry. We start the process with an opening prayer. Mine goes like this: "Holy Spirit, be present and guide every thought, every word, every action that takes place here. This is Your process. You gave it to me. I was your first subject. I thank you in advance for a great result. Amen."

To see and eventually to "see" the potential ahead of us is to admit, "I cannot know this surrendered life, nor can I live it, without an ongoing yielding to the Holy Spirit, hour by hour, day by day, for the rest of my life."

What is it that the surrendered person comes to "see" differently?

- *Life and death*—she views death as merely a "crossing over" and life as a continuous and ongoing process of becoming.

- *Stewardship*—he regards everything as belonging to God, including all that he possesses, all of his time, all of his energy, and the very body he inhabits—the material realm is entrusted to a person for Godly use.

- *Possessions*—he realizes that he does not *own* possessions. Rather, he *owes* possessions. All he has and is belongs to God and must be at His disposal to do with as He desires. The surrendered person soon asks the Master, "How can I put what You have blessed me with—graced me with—to Your highest purpose?" When it comes to the gifts He so freely and generously gives us—natural, spiritual, and supernatural—the response of the surrendered person must always be, "Lord, You own these gifts. How can I use them to Your greatest glory?"

  When it comes to financial resources, the surrendered person soon finds himself praying, "Lord, You have loaned these things to me. What do You want me to keep for myself? Is it really ninety percent? I don't need that to live well. How should I put Your surplus to work, Lord?"

  Certainly surrender does not mean denial of joy, goodness, or appreciation of beauty and God's blessings. Rather, it means that we come to grips with the truth that we cannot become Christ-centered through indulgence. What we deny is not all pleasure, but rather all that constrains us, limits us, or inhibits our witness for Him.

• *Marriage*—the surrendered person sees the family as God's basic building block for His kingdom—for both the procreation of natural children and spiritual children. Having adopted three children I can tell you that the love the Lord God puts in your heart is no less than for natural children. God expands your heart to love all equally. New mothers often say, "How can I love another child as much as I do this first baby?" Then they have the second baby and find out that they can love another child just as much as the first. This is God's way of helping assure that a parent doesn't play favorites. (When they do, it is extremely harmful to the child held in less regard.)

• *Parenthood*—he accepts that children are loaned to their parents by God, and being a parent is a person's highest calling, whether as a natural parent or a spiritual parent, or both. Helping a child get on the path of a transformed life is a covenant that God makes with every surrendered parent.

• *Servanthood*—he acknowledges that all talents and gifts are to be employed for the expansion and development of God's kingdom.

• *Suffering*—he accepts that God can cause good to come from all suffering.

It is in Surrender that a person knows he must be patient in trials and seek to learn what it is that God is teaching him—all suffering and tension are a part of life and are among God's ways of developing, not destroying, His children.

It was critically important in my life that I be in a spiritual transformation phase of Surrender as I faced my wife Ginny's battle against lung cancer. I do not know how I would ever have handled her struggle and the many treatments she underwent—some of which gave temporary relief and even remission but all of which, in the end, failed. I do not know how I would have had the courage to face another day after Ginny died had I not already Yielded fully to the Holy Spirit and had come to "see" the potential of a Surrendered life.

• *God's Word*—the surrendered person sees God's Word as being—*alive!* The surrendered person reads with new, discerning eyes and an increased level of understanding. He quickly comes to the conclusion that a person cannot know God if he does not know His Word. Long ago a wise person wrote, "The Word is your pilgrim's staff, it should fill the memory and rule the heart." The surrendered person has a desire to read God's Word daily to become wise—he believes the Word and lives it. He applies it to his daily life. The Bible becomes the road map of a holy life, the key to knowing what to do and how to live in order to be fully in right standing with the Father.

• *Goals*—the surrendered person has only one overriding goal: all things to God's glory. There is a willingness to embrace whole-heartedly goals that call for us to empty ourselves for others.

• *Self*—the surrendered person sees himself as a completely new, holy person. He has a heightened inner sight and outer sight. He recognizes God's hand at work in all things and recognizes the balance in God's master plan. A man once said to me, "Tom, there are miracles all around me that I hadn't noticed before!" I asked him to give me an example. He said, "Just last week it suddenly dawned on me that animals in the wild drop their young in the spring—that's when food supplies will be ample for the raising of their young. God designed it that way!" He was so enthusiastic about this simple truth that I rejoiced with him at his "discovery!"

I have long been fascinated by the extravagant variety and beauty of the flora and fauna of this earth. God has given us a beautiful, fascinating, wonderful world to enjoy. He wants us to see His hand everywhere. He wants us to know that He cares—even about the smallest details of His creation. He governs all things—and He does so in a way that promotes harmony, balance, and sustenance. I believe every surrendered person has new insights into what, how, and why God does what He does.

"Christ in Me" Requires Ongoing, Unceasing Practice

The age-old adage "practice makes perfect" is true for the spiritual life as well as the perfecting of skills. "Practice" is at the heart of all spiritual disciplines. However, it is perfect practice that makes perfect; imperfect practice reinforces error. Much of surrender comes as we "practice" doing those things that we know with certainty are part of God's plan for us.

Surrender may come in stages—a person may have significant, even memorable "moments of surrender." Usually, however, surrender seems to be a progressive development that comes as a natural byproduct of day-in and day-out decisions, choices, and behaviors. The process is fairly easy to define. Satan comes frequently with his temptations and it is as we say "no" to those temptations that we yield more of ourselves to Christ.

The first eleven verses of Matthew 4 deal with Satan's tempting of Jesus. The point of these passages in the Word is to demonstrate that Jesus is a worthy Savior. He was led into the wilderness by the Spirit. Satan tried three temptations, each of greater magnitude. (Command the stones become bread; throw yourself off the pinnacle of the temple in Jerusalem; "fall down and worship me and I will give you all these [kingdoms].") At this point Jesus had had enough. He told Satan to "be gone," the devil left, and angels came to minister to Jesus. As prince of this world Satan had the right to make this final offer. Jesus was tempted by the master tempter and yet continued to live a sinless life.

We must always remember that temptation itself is not sin. Yielding to it is. As we say no to the devil's temptations (which are choices) and yes to God's commands (obedience is also a choice), we experience a renewal of our minds. New mental, decision-making pathways are developed within us. These new pathways bring about new emotional responses and attitudes, and as we develop new emotional and attitudinal pathways, our spiritual nature changes. We *grow* into the likeness of Christ. Paul teaches us in Romans that God causes all things to work together for good to those who love God, to those who are *called* according to His purpose (Romans 8:28 NKJV). In Romans 8:29 Paul says, "He also predestined to be conformed to the image of His son that He might be the firstborn among many brethren." God builds His Church through an "A" team. As the elect develop, their spiritual nature becomes increasingly Christ-like. You can see Christ in their faces.

It is the height of arrogance to think that the Christ life occurs without effort. When we initially come to Christ, we are far from His likeness, no matter the age or "condition" in which we make that initial decision. Our sins are forgiven in an instant, we move from one spiritual dimension to another, but we are not made perfect in that moment. Jesus used the metaphor of being "born again." The apostle Paul writes of being made a "new creature" and Peter also writes about being "born anew." The birthing of our new spiritual life is very much like the birthing of a baby. There is an ongoing process that lies ahead. Surrendered souls develop at a quickened pace. They have the ability to digest meat in terms of their learning (as opposed to milk).

In like manner, we are "born again" definitively, perhaps even in dramatic fashion, but we are not made mature in that moment. We will face pain, struggle, disappointment, refinement, discipline, and effort as we move toward adulthood—even as a baby faces those things in the normal course of moving through childhood to adulthood.

In many ways, the process is one of alignment with the "life" of Jesus. He is our role model. His character traits are to become *our* character traits. His utter dependence upon His Heavenly Father, and the intimacy He enjoyed with His Father, are to be the hallmarks of the way *we* relate to our Heavenly Father. His sensitivity to doing only what the Father does is to become our sensitivity as we live out Christ's life, using our feet to take us where the Spirit compels us to go, and then using our eyes to see the needs, our ears to hear the Spirit's response to the needs, our mouths to give voice to His words of encouragement, and our hands to do the work that He directs us to do.

In character, in relationship, and in ministry, we are to become like Jesus Christ.

This process of alignment with the likeness of Christ is a learning process. We must learn how to live His life in every situation and circumstance, whether this is the circumstance of dealing with the irritating neighbor next door, the irksome boss or co-workers, the aggravating spouse, or the annoying child. Every encounter and reaction must be intentional, filtered through our highest degree of understanding about what Jesus would do or say if He was walking in our shoes. As we mature in Christ we go through stages akin to the human life cycle: baby, child, youth, adult. But while our physical body wears out, our Spirit can continue developing in conformance to that of our Lord. We don't have to stop becoming increasingly Christ-like.

Some of my clients live in Asian countries. This has provided me a wonderful opportunity through the years to study the work of master calligraphers and master landscape artists, in Japan especially. No person becomes a true master in either of these fields in less than twenty years. I have been privileged to observe masters at work—they work well, very quickly, and almost effortlessly. What underlies that quick, effortless work are years of untold hours of practice at honing the skill.

The same is true for those who are at the top of any creative profession—artists, musicians, authors, actors, filmmakers, and designers. It is true for those who are master craftsmen with wood, metal, stone, fabrics, or other materials. It is also true for those who are highly experienced in making astute business calculations, medical diagnoses, or counseling profiles. It is true for those who become highly skilled in the classroom or adept at conducting seminars or speaking publicly.

Practice produces excellence.

Practice improves efficiency.

Practice brings the best possible results related to performance of skills.

Practice increases speed related to the attainment of desired results.

What does this have to do with the Christ-centered life? Everything!

We Christians go to church for an hour a week, sing a couple of songs, read a few verses from the Bible, and hear a sermon. In some churches, and with varying degrees of periodicity, we have Holy Communion. We bow our heads in prayer and are dismissed. We say we are engaged in becoming more like Christ through this weekly ritual. Frankly speaking, such a conclusion is ludicrous. To be a Christian requires a daily surrender of self and a determined decision to think, speak, and act like Christ Jesus every waking hour of every week. As I have said, only perfect practice makes perfect. I'll use myself as an example. While far from being perfect, I have made a great deal of progress. When I first married, my wife would not share with me the misbehavior of our children for fear of my explosiveness. We tend to replicate the behavior we have experienced at home, even if we hated how a parent treated us or others. We haven't experienced any other role model. Learning a new behavior tends to be a slow process.

Three Wonderful Facets of the Surrendered Life

There are three facets of the surrendered life that I regard as particularly wonderful: accelerated spiritual growth, increased balance and wholeness, and a deeper relationship with the Lord.

• *Accelerated Spiritual Growth.* Although I came to the place of surrender relatively late in my life, I am aware that the transforming process within me has been greatly accelerated during the last fifteen years. During the first thirty years after I initially acknowledged Jesus as my Savior, change in my life was slow. There was very little change in actions, speech, or the way in which I perceived the world around me. Upon conversion, I had received an assurance that my sins had been forgiven and that I was destined for eternal life. But beyond that, I experienced very little change in the way I lived each day from sunup to sundown. I attempted to lead a good, moral life, worked hard, earned a good living, provided for my wife and children as best I knew, and attended church whenever I was in town. In many ways, my decision to become a more loving husband and parent were born out of new information that I gained from academic studies about human nature. It was not a decision I had made that was birthed by Holy Spirit conviction.

Since my surrender, change is something that seems to have happened at a rapid rate. Certain negative lifelong habits simply melted away. Other new Godly habits took root and flourished— *rapidly.* New insights into God's purpose and plan as revealed by the Scriptures have become an almost daily experience.

Immediately after my surrender, my daily routine—including the basis on which I made decisions, accepted clients, and ordered my schedule—became significantly different. I developed new reading habits and my thought life was focused on the consideration of different concepts. My relationships deepened. For the first time in my life, I had an abiding, steadfast, and unquenchable personal peace.

I finally found freedom to be fully myself, even as I had yielded my full self to the Lord. I knew that I had nothing to prove to either myself or to God. God knew me fully, loved me infinitely, and desired to reveal more and more of Himself to me. My vulnerability with the Lord was met with such overwhelming acceptance that I had the confidence to become vulnerable to others. The presence of the Lord, and the keen awareness of His love for me, transformed me so that I could both know myself and love myself as never before—and also be willing to know others and love them as never before.

- *Increased Balance and Wholeness.* All of us want and need happiness. When we are happy, our lives take on greater "quality." We enjoy life infinitely more. We desire wisdom, for with wisdom our life becomes shaped by decisions that result in goodness and blessing. In turn, our children's lives become shaped by our wise counsel—they become the beneficiaries of our wisdom as we influence their thinking and behaving.

A key and often overlooked aspect of happiness, however, is balance. Those who are "whole" are happier than those who are not!

I am always in awe at the way God designed our brains. The brain has a speculative, introspective side that theorizes. This is the side of the brain that intuits and creates. There is also a practical side of the brain that solves problems. This is the side of logic, analysis, reason, and rationalism. Behaviorists refer to "left brain, right brain"—the analytical brain and the intuitive brain.

Should a person have a serious stroke in the analytical side of the brain, that person likely won't be able to balance her checkbook. A stroke on the intuitive side of the brain can cause unexplainable crying spells. Everyone is biased to one side or the other. The analytically dominant brain is generally found in engineers, accountants, surgeons, and attorneys. The intuitive-dominant brain is generally associated with artists, writers, visionaries, and entrepreneurs.

The Christ-centered surrendered person leads a holy life with both sides of the brain working together to give the balance that a God-given mission requires. That is God's design.

- *Deeper Relationship with the Lord.* Our personal relationship with the Lord deepens as we live in obedience to His will. We naturally talk with Him at any and all times, seeking and receiving counsel. Nine years ago, my wife and I moved to Grants Pass, Oregon, from Big Bear Lake, California. I had a brother living there, Don. Meryl had lived there before and wanted to return. We built a home and visited churches. One Sunday we were visiting Bethany Presbyterian Church where Meryl had been a member previously. It was Communion Sunday. I was standing with most of the congregation on the periphery of the sanctuary. As I took the cup God spoke to me saying, "This is your church." I do not remember whether I was talking with Him at the time. I don't think so. He was telling me His will and He knew we were trying to find the right church home. I thank God for His countless graces. I petition Him for help—for ourselves and for others.

The person who is surrendered fully to the Holy Spirit's direction is a person who focuses on the things of God, is led by the Spirit of God, and who prays more effectively because he prays according to the will of God, becomes more and more the Everyday Saint. These truths are reinforced time and again in the New Testament:

- "Those who live according to the flesh set their minds on the things of the flesh, but those who live according to the Spirit, the things of the Spirit." (Romans 8:5 NKJV)

- "For as many as are led by the Spirit of God, these are the sons of God." (Romans 8:14 NKJV)

- "Now He who searches the hearts knows what the mind of the Spirit is, because He makes intercession for the saints according to the will of God." (Romans 8:27 NKJV)

All of those who have written through the centuries about God's spiritual vision for His children have been totally consistent in their message about the attributes and qualities of the surrendered life. They all speak of:

- Freedom

- A transcendent life

- Total trust in Christ

- Power streaming from God's unconditional love as a person submits and obeys

- Living out a mission of God's love in service to others

- Being possessed by God's power, not the possession of our own power

- Making wise choices that aid in the person's progress and effectiveness as a witness for Christ

- Tremendous spiritual growth: This aspect of growth is an important one. At no other stage in a person's spiritual transformation is such tremendous growth evident.

Wise Counselors

Through the course of my spiritual development, I've read certain authors who push me, prod me, pull me, and I return to them again and again. Because they are able to make me think and question, and inspire me with what is ahead on the walk of faith, they become "wise counselors" to me through the pages of their books. Look for your own wise counselors—in the flesh or on the page!

No spiritual writer has influenced me more on the subject of wisdom than Bishop Fulton Sheen. In his book *Lift Up Your Heart*,* he writes: "Our thoughts make our desires, and our desires are the

---

* Fulton J. Sheen, *Lift Up Your Heart* (New York: McGraw-Hill, 1950), pp. 224–25.

sculptors of our days. When one meditates and fills his mind with thoughts and resolutions bearing on the Love of God and neighbor above all things, there is a gradual seepage of love down to the level of what is called the *subconscious*, and finally, these good thoughts emerge of themselves, in the form of effortless good actions."

E. Stanley Jones has also been a great influence on my spiritual growth, particularly on the subject of the freedom we can experience as Christians. In his seminal book, *Abundant Living*, he wrote: "Man is made for freedom but freedom can only come through obedience. When I am disciplined to the Kingdom of God and obey its laws then I am universally free because its area is universal" (page 179).

My third influence, and possibly yours as well, is Oswald Chambers, whom I spoke of earlier. My wife Meryl would jokingly say, "Life is a battle and then you are dead." She had a point. Chambers wrote that "the thing that preserves a man from panic is his relationship to God: If he is only related to himself and to his own courage, there may come a moment when his courage gives out. Panic will never be the result of the one who believes in the absolute sovereignty of his Lord."

Growth and Change as a Surrendered Saint

At conversion, a person acquires an attitude toward Christ. In surrender, a person moves toward *having* Christ's attitude. One's thoughts are no longer her own—they are in the process of becoming increasingly aligned with the thoughts of God. One's concerns and interests are no longer her own—they are in the process of becoming increasingly aligned with the heartbeat of God.

In surrender, we develop a heart large enough to house Him. We become the temple of the living Savior. The New Testament gives us a vivid portrait of growth and change as a surrendered saint: the life of Paul.

Through my years of life I came to these general overriding conclusions about Paul: God's love turned Paul 180 degrees. Paul went from being a passionate hunter and slayer of Christians to being a great preacher, missionary, and apostle. His conversion and simultaneous surrender is the best example I know of the power of God's love to transform a life. Paul became a new man—a *whole* person in Christ Jesus.

Why did our Lord do such a tremendous work in Paul? It isn't for us to know all of God's reasons and whys, but it is easy to see Christ's need for a "Paul" in the first century. Paul's mission was, in today's parlance, to platform Christ. Through Paul, the world received a deeper understanding of the significance of Christ's work on earth. A higher display of Christ's personality was evident, above what the earliest disciples had possessed.

Paul wasn't understood by many people. In fact, it appears that very few truly appreciated him. His gospel of the complete freedom of the believer was rejected by the vast majority who desired the structure of specific formulas and rituals. Even so, the apostle's emphasis on Christ's death, resurrection, and divine nature literally changed the thinking of the Church. The concept of Jesus the Messiah—a concept that was largely Jewish and that included elements of political and social leadership—changed to Jesus Christ the Divine Savior of all mankind, a thoroughly spiritual and worldwide concept that opened divine forgiveness and the gift of eternal life to the non-Jewish world as never before. This truth of Jesus Christ as Savior became the central focus in Christian belief and worship. In Paul's day, the Christian religion was a small sect, one of many sects. A "Paul" was needed to make Christianity what it became, to rise above the pack.

Paul's pre-Christian experience and the dramatic circumstances surrounding his conversion led the apostles to the gospel of grace (see Acts 9:1–31).

Christianity is unique in its theology of grace. Overwhelmingly, the references to grace in the Bible are found in the writings of Paul. God's grace is the foundation of truth embodied in the epistles written with the Spirit guiding Paul's hand. His Letter to the Romans stands as the clearest treatise on Christian theology ever written.

The theology of grace is sequentially:
Multiplying
Sending
Mobilizing
Discipling
Salvation
Fellowship

I have found eighty-one references to grace in the Bible. They cover these six processes.

How is it that Paul knew so much about God's grace? Certainly his convictions did not flow out of the instruction received from the first apostles. Nor did those convictions flow out of Paul's knowledge of Jesus' teachings gained before or after his conversion. In many ways, Paul was "set up" for an understanding of grace by the turning points he experienced *prior* to his conversion experience. These pre-Christ experiences were the backdrop of legalism and ritual that Paul knew to be in sharp contrast to the concepts of grace that became his foundational conviction for the remainder of his life. In confronting Jesus' teachings, Paul came face-to-face with the *Law of Love* and it became the core principle of his faith. His life became a living fulfillment of Jesus' words in Matthew 22:37–39 (NASB): "You shall love the Lord your God with all your heart, and with all your soul, and with all your mind. This is the great and foremost commandment. A second is like it, You shall love your neighbor as yourself."

Paul's understanding of Christ came by direct revelation of the Son of God manifested personally and directly to Paul. Jesus, through His Holy Spirit, counseled, equipped, encouraged, and strengthened Paul. Paul received the promise of the Holy Spirit—that He would be the supreme Counselor and Comforter—just as the first apostles had received that promise. The promise continues to be extended today to all who will believe and receive. Through the Holy Spirit, "Christ in us" becomes a reality, not a concept. It gives us access to experience the fullness of all that God has for us spiritually and eternally.

Paul emphasized the divine life in man as the true Christian life. We are to be released from the bondage of external law to the divine life within us: the Law of the Spirit. We are made right with God through faith, not by keeping some type of external compliance to tradition or ritual or by "being good." Paul fully understood that the death and resurrection of Christ provided him with the ability to know Christ's mind through total surrender.

The Church owes its emphasis on the Savior's death to Paul's teaching. Christ is the Redeemer from sin and our Advocate before God.

Through my study of Paul—which I consider still to be in its early stages even though I have now studied Paul's life for years—I came to understand how God the Father, Jesus the Son, and the Holy Spirit—the Trinity—works in the lives of those who fully surrender their lives to the Lord. I have come to learn how Christ-the-Divine advances His kingdom. It is the surrendered souls who are at the leading edge of the Lord's advances into the realms of darkness. John Wesley once declared, "Give me a hundred surrendered souls and I'll change the world." I have no doubt that he was right.

Paul's life is the perfect case study of a Christ-centered life; Paul truly lived out God's LifePlan for himself. He lived in an incredible manner totally beyond what he could have ever imagined on his own. As a result, Paul's life changed our world, then and now. God did not "fix" Paul, the man who once breathed death threats and death sentences against the followers of Christ. No! God remade Paul into a *wholly new man*, inside and out. Paul let go of *everything* to fulfill a mission only possible by divine enablement. Together Paul, and Christ within him, changed the course of history. And today, with an ever-growing army, the kingdom continues to bring the good news to all nations of the world.

It is the apostle Paul who wrote:

- "We are the temple of the living God; just as God said, 'I will dwell in them and walk among them; and I will be their God, and they shall be My people.' " (2 Corinthians 6:16 NASB)

- "That Christ may dwell in your hearts through faith; that you, being rooted and grounded in love, may be able to comprehend with all the saints what is the width and length and depth and height—to know the love of Christ which passes knowledge; that you may be filled with all the fullness of God." (Ephesians 3:17–19 NKJV)

- "The mystery which has been hidden from ages and from generations, but now has been revealed to His saints. To them God willed to make known what are the riches of the glory of this mystery among the Gentiles: which is Christ in you, the hope of glory." (Colossians 1:26–27 NKJV)

This good news seems almost too good to be true! Yet, it is truth from the God of Truth. You can stake your life—and your eternity—on it. The apostle Paul seems to have had a higher concept of the role of "Christ in us" than any of the original disciples, at least from what we have of their writings and teachings. Paul is the one who presents most completely in the New Testament the concept that Christ is in all who yield their hearts fully to Him.

It seems probable that Paul described the "fully surrendered" life so well because, of all the apostles, he was the one who once had so diligently tried to become perfect through human effort. As a young man he had zealously studied Scripture. He had ardently pursued anyone who seemed to be sinning against the Law, or who seemed to be heretical in the eyes of the religious leaders. Paul's pre-Christ experiences actually prepared him for a complete renunciation of the value of personal merit and pride—he knew fully that self could not produce holiness. Holiness requires reverent submission to the Holy Spirit. This is the only path to holiness. We must become empty of self. His Damascus Road encounter with Christ Jesus, his subsequent blindness—which resulted in his being led by the hand into Damascus, and his healing at the hand of an obedient Christ-centered man named Ananias, were deeply humbling experiences for Paul. These experiences certainly bore fruit, but it was not fruit of Paul's design or timing.

In the years following his conversion, Paul became fully aware of what it means to be vulnerable to the Holy Spirit and to be completely dependent upon God. He yielded fully, allowing himself to be led moment-by-moment by the Spirit. Through his life and his writings, Paul provides us with a perfect "case study" of God's plan for one of His own.

> *Paul could never have imagined the incredible things God had in mind for him. He later quoted Isaiah 64:4 to the believers in Corinth: "Eye has not seen, nor ear heard, nor have entered into the heart of man the things God has prepared for those who love Him" (1 Corinthians 2:9 NKJV).*

The same is true for us.

Until we have fully surrendered to Christ, we cannot begin to comprehend the joy, fullness, depth of meaning, and purpose God has prepared for us. To the Ephesians, Paul wrote that the Lord is truly "able to do exceedingly abundantly above all that we ask or think" (Ephesians 3:20 NKJV).

In "process" terms, the unfolding exceedingly abundant life is what we experience in Surrender.

Have You Surrendered?

Does the description below reflect where you are today?

· Are you a Christian but not experiencing true peace of soul?

· Do you have deep questions about the life you are living? Perhaps you are struggling with your vocation, a coming transition, your marriage, or your family?

- Is the Holy Spirit whispering to your heart in a small, almost imperceptible voice inviting you to draw closer to Him?

- Do you sense that the Holy Spirit is calling you to some "mission impossible"? Do you also sense that He will instruct you in how to accomplish this mission in time?

If you've answered yes to any of those questions, then recognize that the Spirit of God is moving you to a new dimension of spiritual life and maturity. Something is about to be birthed in you, and eventually through you. God isn't trying to "fix" anything. He is creating a *new* you. He wants you to forget the past and is saying to you, "I am trying to create something totally fresh. Only I can make all things new. You are my grand subject."

God is the Creator.

Trust Him to create the new you.

Here comes the hard part. You have to "clear the decks" to allow God to do His creative work in your life. You will have to get your head, heart, and soul into the game. You will need to surrender to Him. That will require giving up 110 percent of your life—in other words, all that you think you have of your life to give and even the part of your life that you aren't sure you have to give. You will need to yield to Him all of your heart, all of your soul, and all of your mind—all that you are, and all that He will help you become.

As I have already stated, surrender happens as an act of the will. It is a choice.

- Are you willing to accept fully "Christ in me" and "you in Christ?"

- Are you willing to yield all to Christ? Does your willingness include a willingness to yield your will in making choices and decisions to His will—in other words, choosing the choices and decisions He has planned for your life?

· Do you really want Christ to anoint you for a mission of sanctified service? Sanctified service is sacred (holy) service to God's glory, service He has gifted and prepared us to perform. It is service wholly within His purpose for our life.

Saying "yes" to these questions is the starting point for full surrender.

If you deeply desire to surrender yourself to God, I strongly encourage you to take these additional steps:

1. Make a list of those things that you need *out* of your life, such as jealousy, greed, pride, resentment. Write out that list. Be specific. Look for God to begin to exorcise these things that are keeping you from complete union with Him. He will cleanse you thoroughly of all that you confess to Him.

2. Outline the relationship you desire to have with God. Again, write it down. Read Micah 6:8 (NKJV)—"He has shown you, O man, what is good; And what does the Lord require of you, but to do justly, to love mercy, and to walk humbly with your God?" The Lord will put you on the path of His will.

3. Do you feel the Holy Spirit nudging you to the next step in your life? Do you feel like getting on your knees or flat on your face? Do you feel something electric moving inside you? I strongly recommend that you put yourself into a position of worship as you claim your birthright as a child of God.

In 1995, the Lord led me to pray the Prayer of Surrender that you find below. Since that time, many people have used this prayer in surrendering their lives to the Lord. You may be moved to do so. Another copy of this prayer is found at the back of this book. You may want to consider signing and framing that copy and placing it where you will see it every day.

Prayer of Surrender

Lord,

You know the entire course of my life, as the Author, Perfector, and Finisher of my faith. You knew me before my conception. I was created by You and born to be free and truly alive. Such a life, however, is not what I have led. I have not been in phase or in alignment with Your will. I know that You are the Way. You have shown me Your path of life.

I want to walk humbly beside You, now and forever. I want to live my life within Your will. I may not always do so—even when I believe I am doing so, I may not be. But, Lord, you know my heart. You will not let me stray.

I am safe in Your love and my heart is to please You. You are my all. I have but one overriding goal: to glorify You, Father. I want to please You with the life I lead for You. Your Word has instructed me in how to live in accord with Your will. Help me to live out Your Word in this world.

Thank you, Father, that You are bringing me to heaven: I am on the path! Thank You for giving me a glimpse of heaven every day I am here. Thank You, Father, for Your fullness of life, full measure, tamped down yet overflowing.

Because I have surrendered, You now live—REALLY LIVE—within me. My heart has infinitely enlarged its capacity to love. I am becoming a reflection of You. I am serving You through my talents. I am crafting them, becoming their master. My life now has great purpose, my mission is clear. I am free, radiantly alive. I look forward to each day of Your grace.

Bless you, Father. Amen.

Do you feel as if something wonderful has happened? Do you feel as though a load has been lifted off your shoulders? Are you at peace?

You are on the verge of becoming best friends with God!

Clothe me with power from on high!

Spirit, I unconditionally submit to Your love.

I surrender to Your presence, asking for Your guidance in all things.

Take possession of my mind, my heart, and my soul.

I will be obedient to Your will, Master.

Your Divine power will work in my weakness.

Glory be to God: I will live out my life under the Highest Power.

chapter 9

Nine Areas of Change and Growth

O*ne of the best ways* a person can evaluate whether he is "progressing" in the stage of Surrender is to look back over the previous six months, year, or a slightly longer time period, and ask, "In what ways am I changing or growing spiritually?"

At times, a person may have difficulty seeing significant change in his or her own life. If that is the case, it is wise to talk to someone who knows your life well, and who has your best interests at heart—ideally, a fellow surrendered believer in Christ Jesus. Ask that person, "In what ways do you believe I am growing, or not growing? In what ways am I becoming more like Christ Jesus, or failing to mature spiritually?

I am a firm believer in, and advocate of, accountability partners. Such a person may be a mentor or spiritual guide. Even if you have no formal mentoring relationship, the person should be more mature in his or her walk with the Lord than you are. It should be a person you seek to emulate spiritually. Above all, the person should love you deeply with God's love and desire that you be in pursuit of God's best and highest for your life. The person should be more concerned about your spiritual growth than your material or career success. Finally, the person should be someone who is willing to be in an accountability relationship with you, and who is accessible to you on a periodic basis that is subject to your mutual agreement.

The surrendered person has a new awareness in nine areas of spiritual development that give rise to tremendous change and growth. Look for spiritual transformation in these areas! Here they are:

A new awareness of God's grace at work
A new desire to know God's word
New devotion to daily work with Christ
Positioning ourselves to sense His presence
Focusing on Christ
An ongoing awareness of God's blessings
Daily prayer
New levels of peace and freedom
A new step toward wholeness

A New Awareness of God's Grace at Work

In surrender we become extremely sensitive to God's grace in our life. Christ begins to reveal to us just how much He has been involved in our days—even before our birth. All of history has been arranged in a precise preparation for our appearance on the earth. God has been at work all along, determining who our ancestors would be, creating step by step the precise genetic code we would have, and creating the exact "inheritance" that would be ours today. God has specifically designed the natural talents and propensities and personality with which we are born, and which do not change. Christ is the *Alpha* of our existence. He is our Creator, and His creative work began in ages past and does not cease after our birth.

Throughout our life, God has been "backstage," preparing events and circumstances and encounters that would result in the Gospel being presented to us. He has wooed us to Himself in sometimes subtle, sometimes dramatic ways.

As we surrender more and more of ourselves to the Lord, He also reveals to us the impact we might have on future generations. It's as if He's pulling the curtain back slowly and in increments we can comprehend and act upon—the ways in which He desires to use our life to change the course of history through one relationship after another. We are an integral part of a progressive and ongoing plan.

The truth is, none of us will ever begin anything. That is part of our finite nature as human beings. No idea is truly original. No invention is ever solely our own. Neither will we ever finish the things we start. Our accomplishments will evolve and develop over time long after we have left this earth. What we do for God with Christ in us is eternal—nothing else is.

What Jesus did on the cross—His sacrificial death for the sins of humanity—is the only definitive work that any person has ever "finished." Redemption was completed in Him. Through the process of surrender, we discover a new acceptance of our role in God's ongoing and everlasting plan.

A New Desire to Know God's Word

The process of surrender brings a person to a place where he wants to study the Bible. He desires to set aside a devotional time of reflection and prayer. He wants to do and say what Christ would do and say, and in order to do so, he must be fully informed as to what Christ said and did when He walked in flesh on this earth. Any sense of "have to" about knowing God's Word is replaced with a "want to."

This desire in no way diminishes the importance of self-discipline. Even the person who is fully surrendered must lead a disciplined life. Actually, the will of man is desirous of such character. Even the free spirit or person with the most "laid back" personality has, at some level, a desire for things to be steady, stable, and sure.

We desire a firm foundation on which to plant our lives. We want what we do to bear the quality of solidity—including the relationships in which love is the hallmark. We want to know that certain people can be "counted on" to be faithful to us—even as we recognize the intrinsic value of being faithful to others.

When someone outside us exerts their will upon ours, we have a feeling of "have to" or "must." When we exert our own will, there is a feeling of "privileged to." In yielding our will to the will of Jesus Christ, we have the Holy Spirit as our ally. He bolsters and shapes our human will so that we come to a position in which we feel both "privileged to" and "required to" simultaneously. It is then that true discipline takes root—we intuitively and naturally engage in the disciplines that are the most productive for genuine spiritual growth. The discipline related to reading and studying God's Word is one such discipline.

Reading God's Word without being open to be inspired by it is useless. It is even worse than useless, for such study develops confusion. The surrendered are those who read God's Word with fresh eyes, discernment, and an understanding that flows from a living relationship with God's Spirit. They come to the Word *expecting* to be infused with knowledge, understanding, and wisdom. They expect to be instructed. Knowledge refers to the acquisition of facts, including those that are eternal truths. Understanding refers to an awareness of ways in which truths or facts work together to form eternal concepts and principles. Wisdom refers to acquiring skills of application—how to "live out" what we have come to know and understand.

Not only does the surrendering person expect to be instructed by God's Word, he expects to be inspired by Scripture.

The word "inspired" is a God-oriented word. It refers to being "in-spirited"—it is God breathing into the person the life truth that has already been breathed into the written Word. Inspired men of old wrote inspired words that inspire us today. It is through the Word, and this process of simultaneous instruction and inspiration that the Author of the text reveals Himself by both spirit and truth. I believe that *all* truly great works of man are Spirit inspired.

New Devotion to Daily Walk with Christ

The surrendered person has a desire to develop a deep, intimate relationship with God. It cannot be otherwise. When a person is truly Christ-centered, then Christ dwells within that person by His Spirit, and the Spirit, Son, and Father are *one*. Hear what Jesus prayed for His disciples and for us: "The glory which You gave Me I have given them, that they may be one just as We are one; I in them, and You in Me; that they may be made perfect in one, and that the world may know that You have sent Me, and have loved them as You have loved Me" (John 17:22–23, NKJV).

The person who is seeking to surrender more and more of his life to Christ is a person who has an ever-increasing "hunger" for a deeper and more intimate relationship with the Lord. The surrendering person seeks to listen with greater awareness, sensitivity, and clarity to the inner voice through which He speaks to us. To listen with greater awareness the surrendering person knows he must "tune out" competing voices and distractions. To listen with greater sensitivity, the surrendering person knows he must listen with the heart, fully aware that the Lord speaks to us through our emotions as well as our ideas and creativity. To listen with greater clarity, the surrendering person knows he must be intentional in choosing to listen to the Lord with full focus.

The phrase "Spirit-led" is used often in some Christian circles. To live out a Spirit-led life is a daily challenge. Perhaps a better phrase is Spirit-filled. Moment by moment the person must consult God with a prayer: "Lord, don't let me think a thought that isn't Yours. Never allow me to engage in an activity that isn't pleasing to You. May I never speak a word that is not Spirit filled."

There are several things that I believe are vital as we put ourselves in a position day by day to hear from the Lord and respond to Him.

Positioning Ourselves to Sense His Presence

When we approach the Lord, we must first place ourselves in a position to sense His presence. For most of us, that means finding a physical place in which we experience quiet, solitude, and peace. For me, the place where I experience God's presence with the greatest awareness is in my garden. When I had a home in the mountains, I had a beautiful Japanese-style garden coupled with the majesty of giant evergreen trees. When I had my first home in Southern Oregon, I had a beautiful "pathway" garden with dozens of species of trees, shrubs, flowers, and ground cover—some of them acquired from overseas. When I lived in a desert climate I created a garden that blended into my environs. Now that I once again live in Southern Oregon, I am creating another peaceful garden refuge.

Every garden I create has these elements: running water, places to sit, a path to stroll, rocky crevices and sloping hills, a variety of beautiful foliage blended together for maximum color and texture every season of the year, and over time, the creation of a long-view vista that makes my garden appear to be seamless with the distant horizon. If weather keeps me from being in my garden, I want to be in a room looking out into my garden.

The garden is not only a refuge and a wonderful creative activity for me. It is also a place where I am humbled in knowing that I may be the "cultivator" of God's creation, but I am not the Creator. I may be the "arranger" of living plants, water, and soil, but I am not the Designer of any of the elements that make up my gardens. I have not designed the principles of growth, the intricacies of design, or the beauty inherent in every living thing that God has made. I have not made every pebble unique. Nor have I had a part in engineering the life cycle and dimensions of any plant or tree. In my garden, I am surrounded by the awesome truth that God is the Source of all things.

He did not create the world and withdraw from it. To the contrary, He remains in control of every aspect of His creation at all times. He is the ongoing provider and protector of what He owns. Including me.

My garden is not a place where noise is welcome, other than the sound of flowing water, the singing of birds, and the occasional buzz of insects. My garden is a place where I can tune out the world and become increasingly aware of the "still, small voice" that I know to be the Lord's.

You may not have a garden. The place where you may sense God's presence may be very different than mine. I know one woman who has a special prayer "chair" in her home. She does not sit in that chair unless she is planning to enter into conversation with the Lord. I know a man who has a special vista point where he stops on his way to work each morning. His hours are such that he often arrives at this spot adjacent to a major road just as the sun is coming up. There, as he overlooks the mountains, valleys, and horizon of a new day, he is acutely aware of God's presence. The traffic behind him is "covered" by soft praise music that he plays in his truck. The Central European Jews have a wonderful custom . . . finding a great tree in a peaceful, open area under which they can not only find shade—but also be alone and pray.

Focusing on Christ

Meditation is the most underappreciated practice of a Christian. It is the act which most internalizes the presence of God. It surrenders our will to His will. It draws its effectiveness from three powers of the soul: memory, intellect, and will. I find it very helpful to meditate on one aspect of Christ's nature, and specifically how this aspect of His nature was manifested during His time on earth. From memory I reflect upon His goodness, His grace; from intellect I think upon His life, His love, His divine nature; from the will I feel myself driven to be evermore like Him. If I could have granted but one wish for every reader of this book, I would wish for each to invest one hour a day in solitary meditation. I've never heard a pastor stress this and I pray for this to take center stage. I also meditate on how Christ might manifest meditation in *my* world. I ask myself, "How would He have related to the people I know? How might He respond to the situations I am facing? And what would I learn about His character from that?"

For example, I might focus on Christ's humility. I might then recall how He knelt before His disciples with a towel and basin of water, intent on washing their feet. I would remember that Peter had difficulty accepting that his Lord would wash his feet. "If you are going to do that you might as well wash my hands and head." Jesus rebuked Peter, saying, "If I do not wash you, you have no part with Me" (John 13:8 NKJV). Jesus washed the feet of all of His disciples. He politely told them that only their feet—the dirtiest part of them—needed to be washed. (Imagine how feet only protected by sandals appeared after a day of walking across dirt roads.) His intent was to show humility, His willingness to be a servant. Jesus gave them an example that He wanted His disciples to follow. Or I might recall the self-sacrificing nature that led Him through a garden of agony to the horrors of crucifixion.

Here are some subjects for your meditation:

SOME ASPECTS OF CHRIST'S CHARACTER

Spirit filled	Luke 23:46
Compassionate	Matthew 15:32
Loving	John 15:12–17
Teacher	John 14:26
Sinless	Ephesians 1:7
Humility	Psalm 34:2
Forgiving	Acts 13:38

Wisdom	I Corinthians 24
Prophet	Deuteronomy 13:26
Exhorting	Titus 1:9
Prays	Luke 11:1
True	Nehemiah 9:13
Faithful	Luke 16:10
Merciful	Luke 6:36
Heart for the lost	Psalm 119:176
Good Shepherd	John 21:16
Obedient	Deuteronomy 4:30
Just	Hebrews 12:23
Benevolent	Joshua 2:14
Self-denying, Self-sacrificing	Matthew 4:1–11
The Eternal God and Creator	Deuteronomy 33:27
Omnipotent	Revelation 19:6
The Lord of all	I Corinthians 12:13
Equality with God	Isaiah 46:5–13
Like us in all things but without sin	2 Corinthians 5:21

As my thoughts turn toward Christ's relationship with me, I might recall the ways in which I have witnessed humility in those who serve Christ, or the ways in which I have most effectively ministered to others as a *humble* servant of Christ. I might reflect upon the ways in which Christ would display humility if He was walking in my shoes on that day—interacting with the people I know I will meet and those I do not yet know I will encounter, and dealing with the situations I know I will face as well as those I cannot begin to anticipate.

Finally, as I contemplate the nature of Christ, I am increasingly aware of various passages of Scripture that relate to this attribute and bolster my understanding of it. Mary, the mother of Jesus, for example, reflected great humility. So did Hannah, the mother of Samuel. Their willingness to humble themselves before the Lord put them into a category of greatness, just as Jesus' humility before the Father put Him into a singular category as the "Greatest Servant of All."

A person might spend all day contemplating the humility of Jesus Christ. The same is true for every one of His character traits. The starting points for contemplation on His nature are numerous. He is perfect, loving, joyful, kind, merciful, forgiving, balanced, stable, persistent and enduring, patient, obedient to the Father, peaceable, gentle, confident, strong, confrontational (without being combative), cooperative (without compromising principle), truthful, honest, honoring, encouraging, rewarding, holy, purposeful . . . the list of positive attributes is beyond exhaustion, I suspect, in any given lifetime.

Furthermore, I have discovered through the years, that even if I am focusing on an aspect of Christ's nature that I have contemplated previously, every act of contemplation seems to take on a unique perspective that is related to new experiences, relationships, or events that have transpired in the meantime. The contemplation of Christ's life is multifaceted and never-ending. And the outgrowth of such contemplation is not only increased wisdom and understanding, but also an outpouring of praise. Although we will never fully grasp the glory of the Lord, he does allow us to capture glimpses of His glory. Praise is to be our response. His is the Kingdom and the power and glory forever!

Certainly the ways in which Christ manifested Himself to us should also evoke great thanksgiving in our hearts. We must never become so "accustomed to" our salvation that we cease to be thankful for it. None of us has done anything deserving of, nor are any of us inherently worthy of, eternal life. Nor are we worthy on our own merits and accomplishments to have an intimate relationship with the Creator of the universe, much less have a relationship with Him that is filled to overflowing with mercy, forgiveness, and love; a relationship with the Lord is not something we want to take for granted.

If we're in a dynamic and growing relationship, this becomes hard to do. The more we discover about Him, the more we want to know. As I began to intentionally and willfully yield my will to Christ's will, there was no need for the Lord to cajole me into a deeper devotional life. I desired it! And the truth is, what we desire, we nearly always pursue. As Rick Warren has said, "What catches our mind, catches us."

The pursuit of the surrendered life is not something I feel forced to "schedule." It is not an interruption to what I would rather be doing. To the contrary, these times of devotion have become the ebb and flow of my life—the center around which everything else must be scheduled. Other activities are an interruption to my communion with Christ—even so, I remain aware of an ongoing communion with Christ that occurs in the doing of other activities. I have a constant "God awareness" that permeates all conversations, all events and activities, and all thought processes.

I believe this is the essence of what Paul expressed when he said we are to be in prayer that is unceasing. Every action, every conversation, every thought, every petition, and every word of gratitude becomes a prayer. Daily contemplation—thinking about God and focusing on His Word and Christ's life—turns a monologue prayer into a dialogue. The more you contemplate, the more open you become to hearing the Father speak to you. Your questions produce His answers. Your thoughts become filled with His insights. The emotions of your heart become the canvas on which He paints His compassionate expressions of care and tender love.

An Ongoing Awareness of God's Blessings

As a day proceeds, I choose to be very aware of the blessings God has and is giving me—a cup of coffee with my caregiver, a nutritious breakfast, a ride on my scooter, a phone call from a grandchild, safety and health through a long day of work. I feel certain there are days in which I breathe a quiet "Thank you, Lord" a hundred times or more. Scripture tells us that the Lord delights in hearing our words of thankfulness and praise. I know that if I focus on praising Him, any issue or problem seems to fade in the light of His glory. I start every day with a thank-you for the life He has given me, this wonderful country, community, and neighbors, and express my love for Him. I thank Him for the people he has surrounded me with, the team which is helping me get done what he wants me to do for Him while here.

Daily Prayer

I pray daily for members of my family, friends, and acquaintances in need. Some of those are people who are on a prayer list at our church. Others have needs that involve tasks the Lord has placed in my path.

The surrendered person finds himself talking to God at any and all times. He is quick to thank and praise the Lord. He puts before the Lord his desires frequently and specifically, and He accepts the Father's answers. 1 John tells us, "Whatever we ask we receive from Him, because we keep His commandments and do those things that are pleasing in His sight" (1 John 3:22 NKJV). There is an implicit assumption here: God can only do His will. I could not have prayed harder or more earnestly for my daughter's healing. In the end, as with Jesus on the cross, it was "Your will be done."

Sometimes the answers to our pleas are direct and immediate; sometimes they come as a still small voice at another time of His choosing. The surrendered person learns to recognize the Father's voice, whenever it comes, however it comes. In my life, I have learned that when He speaks, it is usually very calming to my spirit—His voice evokes tremendous peace and confidence. I am continually amazed that I can bring even a small matter to the Lord and receive direction. He has helped me find my mislaid keys, all but putting them into my hands! He helps me discern what He is doing in the lives of those who come to me for LifePlans. He gives me insights into how to plant a garden that reflects harmony of design for all seasons. He withholds nothing that is good!

Is it so surprising that a good Father answers the cries of his children? Is it so odd that He desires a close relationship with the beings that He created for the express purpose of fellowship? God is not cold or distant. Through surrender a person truly has an opportunity to become best friends with God. He is living in us. He is closer than our heartbeat. Our connection to Him is hot-wired and when we call out to Him, we never receive a busy signal.

New Levels of Peace and Freedom

The process of surrender results in increasing feelings of peace and unity, as well as total freedom in Christ Jesus. These twofold "feelings" of union are like the two sides of a coin—they are distinctive and vastly different, yet inseparably entwined. The surrendering person enjoys an increasing sense of release from bondage as he delves more deeply into relationship with his Savior.

Release! Letting go is an overt action on our part, a decision to dive headlong into the spiritual realm is just as real as if we were letting go of something precious and tangible in the physical realm. "Letting go" means allowing God to select, decide, and mold our life according to His design. He builds, shapes, and fashions. We are His instruments.

Rather than demanding that we submit to Him, God invites us to submit to Him. An acceptance of His invitation is our choice. His plan is ours to claim, but only as we release our claim to our plans! As I have mentioned previously, many people equate release and surrender with loss. If you surrender something, you "give it up." For example, in a military action, surrender traditionally and historically has involved the waving of a white flag. The enemy thus "gives up" the fight.

Surrender of self to God is not waving a white flag. It is yielding control in order to team up with the Infinite for a full and eternal victory! Surrender is an alliance—rooted in an alignment—with the God who controls all and therefore governs all, and therefore can protect all and provide all. Surrendering to God's will is a yielding of will, not an abandonment of will. A person maintains her will—it is the key to exercising her faith. The will, however, is subjected or submitted to the infusing power and wisdom of the Holy Spirit so that what we will becomes what has already been willed for our maximum benefit and eternal good!

That's why we can be bold in proclaiming that when we know that Christ is in us, we cannot fail! There is nothing His love cannot conquer. Faith that flows from God will ultimately triumph, no matter how pressing, oppressing, or depressing a current situation might be.

The surrendering person has a feeling of self-abandonment—not to the whims, fates, or fickleness of an amorphous cosmos, but rather, to the One who is all-wise and all-loving. This feeling of self-abandonment is not a feeling of defeat or insignificance, as the world so often portrays it to be. Rather, self-abandonment results in the person "letting go" of self in order to embrace God's greater purpose. The embracing of God's fullness is replete with gratitude and joy. What a privilege to be in perfect harmony with the will of God, and to know that you are part of something so much more grand and eternal than anything you might do out of your own finite and fragile resources. Surrender is reverent submission to God.

Deep and abiding peace comes when one no longer feels anxious, worried, or bound by fear. With that peace, born of union with God's purposes and plans, comes great freedom. You are experiencing Divine Peace: Peace of Soul.

A New Step Toward Wholeness

The person who is on a path toward full surrender of his life to Christ is the only one who has an opportunity for a truly integrated self—becoming whole, complete—functioning as he was designed to function. He has found "wellness" by becoming indwelt by the Source of Wholeness. The more a person yields to the Divine Physician at work within, the more the Lord has freedom to do His healing work. The more a person surrenders, the more vibrant the tone of life itself.

This does not necessarily mean that the flask is unbroken or un-marred. The physical is always ultimately subject to the decay of the physical world that has been marred by sin for untold millennia. The life with the flask, however—the sweet new wine of Christ's own presence—becomes fuller and richer and more robust as surrender becomes more complete. Life takes on a flavor and a quality of exhil-aration as never before. Even as the flesh sloughs away in weakness, the spirit soars with strength.

Surrendering is the key to a person's experiencing true joy, peace, and fulfillment in life. As long as a person is pursuing joy, peace, and fulfillment on his terms and on the basis of her own abilities, intel-ligence, and skills—in other words, facing life with an "I must make it happen" attitude—she will be frustrated and disappointed at every turn, only enjoying a small measure of what the Lord promises.

The person who seeks to drive and define his own life will eventu-ally find himself the victim of his own deep-seated striving. He will feel as if he must continually engage in a struggle against all forces perceived to be obstacles or opponents. There is no more confining way to live than to live within one's own fears, anxieties, and wor-ries. I believe, however, this is how most American adults live.

It is a tremendous burden to be responsible for every success and failure in life, and over time, that burden becomes onerous. There is no more imprisoning way to live than to be shackled by burdens related to one's own success. The more a person experiences "Christ in me and through me," the more a person recognizes that Christ is responsible not only for the goals that are set, but for the ability to achieve those goals. He begins to recognize that Christ is the source of all benefits and rewards. All ability, insight, giftings, talents, and skills flow from Christ. Reaching a goal and all the accomplishments and benefits therein are according to His timetable, His agenda, His purposes, and His enablement. To live with the certain knowledge that you cannot fail is to live fully alive, to live with peace of soul, to live a worry-free life.

The converted person may gain perspective as he matures,
but he remains in an ongoing struggle between self and Christ.
Their thought is, "Let's see if this works to my benefit."
The surrendered person will regard God's plan from
a radically different perspective:
"I know God's way will be for my highest good."
As Thomas Merton once wrote:
"You do not possess your being in yourself but only in Him
from Whom it springs. By faith, I find my own true being in God."*

* Thomas Merton, *Thoughts in Solitude* (1958; repr., Boston: Shambhala Publications, 1993).

chapter 10

Surrendering Every
Dimension and Domain

F*or more than thirty years,* I have been doing LifePlans for people from many walks of life. A LifePlan is a balanced study and projection of someone's life—it allows a person to gain perspective on his past and insight into his God-given talents, personality, dreams, desires, and spiritual gifts. The goal is to help a person make wise decisions about the future—in all areas of his life. People from numerous states and nations—from executives and pastors to people in various professions facing so-called "midlife crises" or "retirement crises"—have come to sit with me for two to three days, solely to focus on who they are in Christ Jesus and where they are headed.

LifePlans are bathed in prayer and are intended for the Christian believer. Indeed, the LifePlan process is a believer's process and is directed by the Holy Spirit. Only the converted person has the enlarged capacity to be fully aware that God has a purpose for her life. Only the surrendered person can make a commitment to living out God's LifePlan . . . and follow through on that commitment.

The process begins with a person completing a number of modules taken from my book *Living the Life You Were Meant to Live.* (There's information on how you can obtain a copy.) The first day we spend together is devoted to developing a "Life Perspective" based upon information gleaned from the completed modules. The Life Perspective helps a person answer such questions as:

- Who am I?

- What are my gifts?

- What drives me?

- What are my roadblocks?

- How did I get to where I am right now?

- How does my past contribute to God's plan for my future?

The Life Perspective portion of the process makes it abundantly clear to the person that God has always been present and active in his life.

A key aspect of this day is devoted to identifying "Turning Points" in the person's life. The result is a "Turning Points profile." Turning Points are significant moments in a person's life in which the person either comes closer to God or turns away—turning toward God's plan for her life, or moving away from it. It may be a period of great suffering, and if it is, God will make good come from it if the person turns toward Him and toward the plan and purpose God has designed for the person. The traumas that result from sin, and a growing yearning for peace of soul, are eventually what bring a person to the point where he throws himself at the Lord's feet and cries, "Father God, I can't handle life by myself. Take my life and use me as You will. I want to serve You. I am desperate for You, Your comfort, Your affirmation, Your guidance, Your love." I came to that point and cried these words to our Lord.

When a person chooses to pursue his own life plan rather than God's he sets himself up in opposition to God. He enters into an argument with his Creator. He is in rebellion. What a mistake it is to argue with God as though we might bend Him to our own way and will! He sees into eternity and knows all things about us. How dare we argue with the One who has such a supreme advantage of information!

Furthermore, God loves us far more than we can ever love ourselves. How dare we argue with the One who has our highest good as His motivation! His will for each of us is our perfection. He calls us to a new awareness and embracing of the truth that we are created in His likeness and are called to become Christ-like.

Fortunately for us, the Lord loves us far too much to yield to our arguments or take our "No, thank You. I'll live life on my own terms" as a final statement. God continues to pursue us. He uses our decisions and choices to bring us to the point where we are willing to say with an open heart, "I can't do this. Forgive me. This isn't working. I need Your help!"

The choices we make will determine if we will yield to God's purposes sooner or later. If we surrender ourselves to Him early, we can live out our earthly existence with many years of maximum fulfillment, purpose, meaning, joy, peace, and ministry. This certainly is God's highest desire for us. Much more will be accomplished in God's kingdom, greater good done, and more blessings received.

A Turning Point Profile often gives witness to the struggle the person has had before coming to a Christ-centered life. A review of life's turning points can also reveal that what were perceived as "disasters" were actually events used by God to prepare a person for her next season of life.

One thing I have concluded in doing literally hundreds of these LifePlans in the last three decades is this: Although a person may have a free choice to receive or resist God's plan, God ultimately has His way in the lives of His people. He is the Creator and He has sovereignty over His creation. He often "hedges" a person to the point that the person is led, step by step, to the conclusion that God knows what is best and God can be trusted to work all things for our eternal benefit.

As I said earlier, I believe the "elect" form the core around whom God builds His kingdom on earth. Others are entirely free to choose; the elect, however, *will* come to surrender for it is vital to the mission God has for them. They can obey early or they can obey late, but they will obey. To ignore God's call, for His elect, takes open, defined rebellion—when the hounds of heaven are upon you, you either fight them off or succumb, right? (Need a biblical example? Think about how He got Paul in His corner.)

God knows His elect by name. He instructs, corrects, and perfects His elect. I would have given my life without hesitation, in exchange for God sparing Debbie's life, or Ginny's. But it was Debbie's illness that started me on the road to absolute surrender. Ginny's illness brought about my unconditional surrender. In prayer I told Ginny I would love her forever, and from the other side she replied, "I will love you forever, but this is your time with Meryl; now take care of her." Meryl has now gone to the other side (1 Corinthians 15:1–13), but I live knowing that I will see all my loved ones again. Surrender to God's plan and believe that He is working through all things for good.

Identifying the Major Turning Points of Your Life

How do you know when something is a turning point and not just a "change" in your life? Here's the sole criterion: The future is *not* the same as the past once you have passed through a turning point. In looking back, you see that you are moving in a certain direction, then something happened that altered your course and changed your life in some way. Certain things of your past may have been dropped or significantly altered; other things may have been strengthened or emphasized. A turning point is not necessarily an event, although that may be the case. Many people have fifteen to twenty turning points by the time they reach age fifty. Spiritual conversion, a marriage or divorce, a birth or death in the family, going to college, the loss of a job, retirement, or a diagnosis of a terminal disease may all be turning points. A turning point is either toward or away from God and His plan and purpose for our life. Conversion and Surrender are major "supra" turning points. The birth of my daughter Debbie was for me . . . as was her death. Every child is not a turning point. To be sure, every child is special, a gift, but what I ask is this: Did the child's arrival draw you closer to God or make you turn away from Him? If it made you do either, it was a turning point.

God's call is always a turning point. Mother Teresa received God's call to be a nun at age eight; at nineteen, she became a nun and was called to India. She taught school in India for upwards of two decades and then on vacation, on a train heading for Darjeeling in the cooler mountains, she received "the call within the call" (her words). She said, "The message was quite clear. It was an order. It was to leave the convent. God wanted something more from me. He wanted me to be poor and love Him in the distressing disguise of the poorest of the poor." Everything about her life changed.

A turning point needs to be evaluated as a change of some type that brought the person closer to God or caused the person to move farther away from Him. As such, a turning point inevitably draws a person toward something that is God-approved or "good" for his life as a whole, or it moves the person toward something that is God-disapproved or "bad" for his life as a whole. A person who becomes converted or makes a full surrender late in life can usually chart the turning points fairly readily because the person has lived to see the outcome of the decision.

Age may bring some measure of perspective. But a key aspect of perspective is seeing things in true relationship. The unconverted (and those who have not surrendered) do not see things with an eye on the bigger picture—that we are God's children, given a life to bring Him glory. The unconverted lead a counterfeit life. Those who believe but have not surrendered lead a half life.

Surrendering Your Past

The critical point I want to convey to you about turning points is this: It is important that you identify the key decisions that you have made in the past and the consequences associated with them. Why? Not only do these turning points give you important information about how and why you live your present life the way you do, but it is important that you *surrender* these past decisions to the Lord. I frequently hear statements such as, "I shouldn't have married that person," "I made a mistake in choosing that career path," or "I should have started going to church sooner than I did."

I always respond, "We cannot rewrite history, but we can make sure we learn from it."

What does it mean to yield your turning points to the Lord? It means that you say to the Lord, "I can see that You were involved in my life all along and that truly, You have and are working all things from my past toward the good of my future. I realize that You were backstage in my life all along, wooing me and moving me toward You. I refuse to hold on to self-blame or to blame others for my past. I choose instead to forgive myself and others, even as I receive Your forgiveness."

We Must Surrender Both the Good and Bad

Many people find it easier to let go of the bad parts of their former life than the "good" parts. If you can't yield the triumphs of your past, your glory moments can become points of pride that keep you from yielding completely to the Holy Spirit. So many Christians today continue to dwell in the memory of old miracles, the "heydey" of old fame, and the accomplishments of former days. As long as they do so, the Holy Spirit truly cannot do a "new work" in that person or through that person.

The disasters of our past can also become blocks. Turning points that were very painful can become areas of bitterness, resentment, anger, and frustration that keep a person from moving forward in freedom to follow the Holy Spirit's leading.

Either way—triumph or disaster—the past must be surrendered to God! Had I not been able to surrender Ginny's death to the Lord— very specifically, surrendering to the Lord any bitterness, resentment, anger, or grief that I felt at her passing—I would not have been in a position to embrace new feelings of love for Meryl, whom God brought into my life. In this case, my love for Ginny did not cease. What *did* come to an end were feelings of struggle, nagging doubts, loneliness, and fears related to her illness and death, and subsequently, my future without her. Those were the residual aspects of this particular turning point that were not in keeping with the surrendered life; I needed to yield them to the Holy Spirit for His healing.

We must not hold on to the best of who we once were if we truly hope to gain the best of who God has designed us to be and seeks to empower us to be. We must not hold on to the worst of who we once were if we truly hope to be renewed, restored, and reshaped to fulfill the purpose for which we were created.

I often speak of practice as it relates to the gifts God has given us. In truth, many people I've encountered "practice" their past mentally and emotionally. They continue to rehearse past statements, experiences, relationships, and decisions over and over in their minds and hearts. The haunting, echoing messages of the past become something of an endless-loop tape playing deep within them. What occupies the mind becomes what occupies time. Beliefs, attitudes, and emotions deep within give rise to behaviors. What we rehearse internally eventually erupts in what we display externally.

I frequently meet people who believe that "practice makes perfect." It does not. Imperfect practice produces great error! Only perfect practice leads to perfect mastery. If we continue to rehearse mental, emotional, or spiritual error, we continue to live in error. And to be certain, anything that was not fully redeemed and transformed by the Lord has an element of error in it. Even our most noble pre-Christ thoughts, words, and deeds are tainted to some degree by our sinful nature. It is only when we release the past completely to the Lord that He has the freedom to write a "new law" on our hearts and minds. It is that "new law" of love, forgiveness, and abiding joy in His presence that must become what we practice! It must become what we dwell on internally.

Surrender the past to the Lord and move into the present with Him.

Surrendering the Present

The LifePlan process calls for a person to recognize that life has "domains," very specifically:

- Personal life—the domain of self,

- Family life—the domain that includes parents, spouse, children, and influential extended family members,

- Church/kingdom life—the domain in which a person relates to others within the Body of Christ,

- Vocational life—the domain of work or career, including volunteer service for which one has responsibility, and

- Community life—the domain in which a person relates to the community at large—usually one's neighborhood, town, or city.*

For some people, such as pastors, the areas of church/kingdom life and vocational life may overlap. Pastors typically cannot separate three of these domains: church/kingdom, vocation, and community. What do I do then? Make a plan for the combined domain. Pastors have great difficulty with the personal life domain. They

---

* I've had a few people for LifePlans whose community was the national stage or the world theater. This was their community.

typically feel they don't have a personal life. Elected political figures may find that community life and vocational life overlap, and so forth. All commitments, responsibilities, activities, and relationships fall into these domains of life.

The key word that must be emphasized in dealing with domains is this: *balance.*

What we need to recognize as a surrendering believer is that (1) our giving and receiving in *every* area of our life should glorify God, and (2) that all areas of life need to be balanced for wholeness so that the totality of a person's life glorifies God.

The Holy Spirit heals, restores, and makes whole. The Spirit moves against imbalance and weakness at all times. He convicts, prods, and compels the surrendering believer to make adjustments that promote the balance and wholeness necessary for a truly effective, efficient, godly life.

There is no provision made in the surrendered life to become totally absorbed in activities and relationships that fall into the church/faith kingdom domain to the exclusion of family or personal life. God receives no glory from a person who mistreats his family, abuses his body, devotes all of his energies and talents to the workplace, or spends so much time contributing to the community at large that he forgets to spend time with the Lord. To the contrary! God receives glory when we are whole, balanced, and healthy in every domain of our life.

The surrendering believer must surrender *every* aspect of the present to the Lord.

Timewise, most of us do not know how we are investing our day. That is, we *really* don't know in any detail unless we track it.

Time Management Model

Here is my proven Time Management Model. Usually, it is most desirable to develop your model on a representative month basis.

Assume
    Twelve hours in a day*
    Seven days in a week
    4.33 weeks in one month
    Therefore: a model month has 364 hours

Life domain	Typical hours/ month invested in domain (hours)	Percent of month invested in domain (%)	Notes
Personal			
Family			
Faith/church			
Vocational			
Community			
Totals (364 hours=100%)	364	100%	

---

* Why twelve hours per day? A workday is normally eight hours; the remaining time is for meals and getting to and from work. Perhaps you are working sixteen hours a day. OK, but stay with the 364 hours per month. You'll see very little time left for your personal or family lives.

Now let's look at a life way out of balance:

How I Invest My Time: A Typical Month

Life domain	Typical hours/month invested in domain (hours)	Percent of month invested in domain (%)	Notes
Personal	25	5%	
Family	29	7%	
Faith/church	10	3%	
Vocational	300	85%	
Community	0	0	
Totals (364 hours=100%)	364	100%	*I had no idea that my family life was only 7% of my time.*

This chart represents my life for over four decades. Next to no time for family, none for community. I came home on Friday nights when I became a consultant in 1970. I left on a plane Sunday afternoon for the East Coast or overseas. A life totally out of balance. Ginny once said to me rather wistfully: "Tom, you are giving me too much room."

Now make your own model. First, what is the present reality? Use the template above.

Ask yourself which life domain dominates your life weekly. Fill out the times and percentages per month in the chart on page 186. Next insert the remaining domains.

Can you see where realignment is needed?

Surrender your own personal desires, health, and intellectual pursuits to the Lord. Ask Him to be Lord over what you eat, what you think, what you dream about, how you exercise, what you choose to do for fun, and so forth. There is no aspect of your physical, emotional, or intellectual self that is outside the boundaries of full surrender.

Surrender your family life to the Lord. Ask Him to be actively present in all of your family's comings and goings—to reveal to you ways in which your family life might be rebalanced for wholeness, and show you ways in which to honor your spouse and children.

Surrender your work or career to the Lord. Ask Him to be your agent and your ally—to bring to you the work that you are suited and equipped to do, and to bring you into relationships that can make your work highly productive and beneficial to others. Ask Him to show you how to infuse all that you do with quality.

Surrender your church work to the Lord. Ask Him to guide you clearly into how you might best become a healthy contributing part of His greater body of believers. Nothing the Lord leads you to do will be in conflict with other believers or detract from the employment of their gifts. Everything He leads you to do will be a blessing not only to you and your family, but to others in your faith community.

Surrender your community service to the Lord. Ask Him to reveal to you which clubs, associations, activities, and events are part of His plan for you, and then say no to every other commitment that others might attempt to foist upon you.

Above all, surrender the "whole" of your commitments, agendas, and schedules to the Lord. Ask Him to show you His plan for balancing your life and producing greater wholeness. Ask Him to reveal to you areas where you need greater input, and areas in which He desires that you give greater output.

At this point I have facilitated more LifePlans for pastors than anyone else—more than four hundred, so far. Typically their life is very imbalanced. Most pastors do not understand what a personal life is because they do not have one. One pastor I met with had a growing church in a major southwest city. He had had three near death experiences. With one he was hospitalized for six weeks. His congregation loved him but the job was killing him. His LifePlan called for him to stop being a pulpit pastor. His heart was in training and teaching educators. For some years now he has been doing just that on the East Coast. His life is balanced. He and his family are very happy and his health restored.

A senior pastor at one of our nation's largest churches came for a LifePlan. It became clear that ministering to the very ill and counseling the bereaved was killing him. His heart and God's purpose for him was in administration. He left on Friday with a plan to become executive pastor in charge of administration. His pastor-leader readily agreed and on Saturday, the next day, he called me to tell me he had his new job. "You are talking, Tom, with the happiest man alive." The church has more than doubled in size and he now has an administrative staff of five senior pastors. (Put the right person in the right job and all the problems melt away.)

Balance and wholeness in every domain. That's at the heart of surrendering your present to the Lord. Do not think this is easy. It is not.

You might be wondering how I rebalanced my life. When we adopted three young children at age forty-five, I vowed not to make the same mistake twice. I wish I could say I did a great job of rebalancing. But I did do better by our second family. They got about 15 percent of my month, up from 7 percent. What gave way? Vocation.

Surrendering Your Future

The LifePlan process culminates in exercises that answer this question: What is God's plan for my future? The subset of questions includes:

- What do I want my life to look like five years in the future?

- What is my current status with this model?

- What actions am I going to take to move me toward my objectives?

These questions are asked for each life domain.

God wants each of His children to lead a balanced, righteous life organized around what really matters, not only for the present day and immediate future, but for all eternity.

In many ways, the surrender of our future to the Lord is a request that He give us a new perspective about our life and what might still be done by us to extend his Kingdom on this earth.

In the corporate world, we often asked questions such as these as part of strategic planning sessions:

- What are the patterns and trends shaping the future of our field?

- What are the opportunities we see?

- What are the risks?

- What are the constraints?

- If we do not change some things, where will we end up?

- Are we on a success track?

- Is the emerging reality going to be a failure?

For decades I spent countless hours helping corporate leaders see both the present and the future with clarity—and when it came to the future, to see it with such clarity that it appeared to be a present reality. I wanted them to be able to feel and taste the future as if it were in their grasp right now.

I believe the Holy Spirit delights in doing exactly the same thing for the surrendered believer. He gives the surrendering person a glimpse into her own future, and He allows His dreams and visions for what the future might hold to come to the surrendered person's conscious mind. He especially holds out those things that He desires to be the "evidence" for faith—the accomplishment of goals and plans that are of His design and definition. These truly are the things "worth believing for."

Are you willing to surrender your dreams and hopes, your aspirations and ambitions to the Lord? *Surrendering your future to God is vital if you desire to experience the fullness of all that He desires to bestow upon you.*

A Whole Life That Is Wholly Christ's

One of my favorite New Testament verses related to God's plans for us is from the writings of the apostle Paul: "In Him also we have obtained an inheritance, being predestined according to the purpose of Him who works all things according to the counsel of His will" (Ephesians 1:11 NKJV).

All of us are called to be ministers, to someone in some way. The fully committed Christian—the fully surrendered Everyday Saint—desires to be mastered by the Lord. He desires to have the Lord direct all that He becomes and does. He is willing to yield *all* his heart to the Lord and to become the slave of Christ—at His beck and call, night and day, to do whatever He commands. His command will always include sharing Christ's love and mercy. In this, then, we become "ministers" of Christ.

We serve our Lord's highest purposes
when we offer our gifts for His service.
In offering Him gifts He first gave to us
we will know God's joy, the abundant life
He has promised.
We become best friends with God
as we walk His path with Him.

chapter 11

Surrendering Our Gifts

One of the foremost things that we surrender to the Lord are our *gifts*—our talents, innate abilities, desires, drives, and dreams. I believe a desire that is a longing is a strong indicator of a gift. An intense dream may be as well. Singer invented the sewing machine while he slept. When he awakened he put a detailed working design on paper. In helping a person find his giftedness I always ask: "What do you long for? What do you dream about becoming?" I dreamed about becoming the best business development person in our country. As I write these words, at the age of eighty-four, Cambridge Who's Who has just informed me that they have selected me as the Business Development Person of the Year for the United States. God uses our dreams and desires to nudge us toward the purpose He has in mind for us. We are called to serve God through our innate abilities (Romans 12:4, 5, 8).

The only things we can truly master in our life are our talents. The gifts we have been given by God are a major key to living a fulfilled life in Christ—they are at the core of our serving Him in a way that has maximum purpose for us and maximum effectiveness in the lives of others.

Our gifts are a manifestation of God in us. In reality, they are His gifts. He has put these gifts in us for His purposes. Many people are not in possession of themselves. When you discover your gifts you have found yourself. You will know the areas to focus on for your growth.

Discerning Gifts

Many people don't know who they are. They haven't found themselves. The key to realization about who you are as God's creation—both at home and at work—is to discover your gifts. You can be a great help to your children in guiding their careers if you help them come to grips with their talents. Show me a person with little sense of purpose or value, and I'll show you a person who doesn't know who he is; his gifts are unknown, undeveloped, and are not being used in service to others. Gifts are a manifestation of God in us. They are part of His infinite and glorious Self, implanted in us for His purposes.

Passions are a major clue to gifting. A passion is what you cannot get enough of, what you want to do forever. *Passions make work play.* I am passionate about strategic planning. I've made it a career for fifty-plus years now and it never felt like work. Some other examples of passions are designing, creating, composing, healing, and preaching. Ask yourself:

- What do I love to do?

- What can I *not* imagine living without or never doing again?

- What makes a day or an experience complete to me?

Winston Churchill said, "When I get to heaven, I want to spend the first thousand years painting." That's a passion.

Drives are compulsions. I am opportunity driven. I am always looking for new ways a concept might be applied. My wife Ginny was need driven. She was an R.N.—practical, problem solving, and a great nurse, able to discern needs quickly and before they became overwhelming. Ginny was great at diagnosis and was often sought out by mothers in the neighborhood, seeking advice about their sick children. Her sister, Sandy, brought her sick baby to Ginny. Ginny took one look, saw that the child was dying and took them in her car, running stop signs and red lights to get to the emergency room. She saved her nephew Stephen's life.

Obsessions are something a person feels compelled to do or have; without the desired object, relationship, or accomplishment, life has little meaning or quality for the person. Examples of obsessions include fame, power, control, wealth, usefulness, and contribution. Ask yourself:

- What do I seek to possess, do, or give at all costs? (It may be spiritual, intellectual, emotional, or material.)

- To what do my thoughts and desires inevitably seem to turn again and again?

Obsessions may be unhealthy or healthy. Monet had a magnificent obsession with water lilies. Patrons built him a retreat with a home, and a pond with water lilies. He lived out his life there happily painting. In my opinion, no painter has ever even approached the beauty of Monet's water lilies.

Characteristics are traits that others see almost immediately in you. They are both inner (emotional, spiritual) and outer (physical, behavioral) qualities. Some examples are being talkative, energetic, quick-witted, slow talking, or self-righteous.

Qualities are traits innate to you, the product of what you have become or are becoming. They are your inner core. Examples are always giving 100 percent, dedication, being outgoing, relational, trustworthy, a team player. Ask yourself:

- If a close friend were to describe me in one word, what would that word be?

- What trait do I look for above all others in a friend or associate?

Needs include the common basic requirements all of us have for food, water, air, shelter, and security, but we also have a need for meaning and purpose in life. Beyond this, each of us has needs unique to us. I need a fair amount of orderliness, music, and time in my garden. Some of us need to work alone. Examples are affirmation, encouragement, new challenges, personal space, love, and being outdoors. Ask yourself:

- What do I need to feel if I am able to fully function?

- What types of rewards do I need?

- What makes something worthwhile to me?

Longings are yearnings, or unexpressed deep drives or whispers of secret prayer. Often in a LifePlan the subject exclaims, "Never before have I verbalized this, even to myself." You may have felt this longing for years. Yearnings and longings are much deeper than dreams or goals, they underlie dreams and goals. They may be symptomatic of a deep inner dissatisfaction, often with a career.

People operating within their God-given purpose seldom think of retirement. The person who has a strong dream of retiring should explore this yearning, not so that he can retire, but so he can start doing what he truly loves to do. I have often seen a yearning for more time with family. It is the unusual LifePlan that doesn't need a rebalancing in the subject's life. With gentle probing I have often brought to the surface a yearning in which the result was my "giving permission" to incarnate the yearning. Examples of yearnings are to be free, to be self-determined, to be respected, and to be part of something. When I finished a strategic plan in Canada, one of the people in the group stood up and said, "I have been with this company for more than twenty years and this is the first time I feel like part of it." His input was heard—his longing was to feel a part of his own company. Ask yourself:

- What do I most wish I had in my life that I do not presently have?

- If I could add just one more accomplishment to my life, what would it be?

- What would I most like to do, change, or try?

Hopes could also be called expectations. Expectations are what you expect the future to hold for you . . . where you hope you end up. Examples of hopes include getting ahead, retiring gracefully, having your employer invest in your development, recognizing growth and opportunity in a company, and a closer relationship with your children. Ask yourself:

- What do I hope to do in my life?

- What do I hope to be?

- What do I foresee as areas of future growth and accomplishment?

- What type of Christian, friend, spouse, member, or participant do I believe I *should* be?

Ginny said to me as she was dying, "I had far more than I ever expected to have." That statement has become a golden moment in my life. I had never thought that she had many expectations, or hopes, but she obviously did. It warmed my heart to know I exceeded hers.

Achievements are personal and vocational accomplishments of which you are proud. These are strong indicators of who you are and the gifts you have. They reflect what you are equipped to do. Even awards or victories that you consider minor can be good indicators of gifts. Examples of personal accomplishments include peer recognition, election to office, a successful marriage, achievement of a college education while working (one of mine), and service awards. Examples of vocational accomplishments include a successful start-up, chairing a task force that fulfilled its mission, a track record of growth, and employee awards. Ask yourself:

- What is my foremost accomplishment to date (in my opinion)?

- What have I done that I believe is worthy of distinction or honor?

Figuring Out Your Gifts

I have given you nine categories of clues and questions to ask yourself in each category. Number your answers consecutively. Now take a sheet of paper, one for each category of clues. Write down the questions, leaving space to fill in your answers. Don't rush this. When you have answered all the questions, deduce what your answers are trying to tell you about your gifts. Do not take something directly out of your answers. Go over your answers, asking, "Which answers are firm evidence of a specific gift?" In the end you should not have over four gifts. Firm evidence would be to have at least fifteen hits out of the twenty questions.

In my LifePlan process, "talents" is the module that most requires professional help. It is very hard for people to get all their gifts correct. A person is too close to see it. Nevertheless, the person who does this "homework" always gets some of it correct. And, it is a big help to a facilitator if you wish to pursue this further. If you need help, and you don't have access to a LifePlan facilitator, ask a friend to go through the questions with you. Sometimes, a trusted confidant can help you see things more clearly.

Years ago an organist in a church in Germany played a lifeless, aimless version of a Bach fugue as an opening prelude. At the end of the service a little old man came to the altar and asked the organist if he might play the organ for a few minutes. At first the organist refused, thinking, *If I let him play, everyone will want to do this in the future.* But something about the old man made him finally say, "Go ahead and play. I'll be gathering my music for a few moments."

The old man began to play that same fugue. But this time it had brilliance, color, nuance. The organist was stunned. He sat down in the front pew and listened. When the old man was finished the organist, in a reverent voice, said, "Sir, who are you?" The man replied, "I am Johann Sebastian Bach and I wanted you to hear my fugue played as I meant it to be played."

As a poor young man, Bach walked two hundred and fifty miles carrying his suitcases to study under his great teacher, Johann Pachelbel. You can hear Pachelbel's influences on Bach in Bach's music. Bach had developed his talent into superb skills through applied practice under the tutelage of a master teacher. There is no substitute for training and practice in any field or for any talent.

The second thing to keep in mind, when considering what it means to master our gifts, is that perfect practice has a "character" quality to it. I have heard a number of outstanding pianists in my lifetime. I admire those who can play the piano or organ with excellence—there is an ease and a fluidity about the way they play. But I have heard twenty-year-olds with great technical excellence play a difficult concerto flawlessly—with their fingers always hitting the right notes at exactly the right time—and I have heard a seasoned sixty-year-old play the same concerto, also flawlessly and with technical excellence. But the two performances do not sound the same. The one played by the seasoned sixty-year-old has an added dimension of sensitivity and musicality to it that is difficult to define but nonetheless real. I have also had the opportunity to hear such a concerto performed by a seasoned sixty-year-old who has loved the Lord Jesus Christ for many decades. Never have I heard more beautiful music!

This man plays the piano with no greater technical ability, no greater sensitivity and musicality than another skilled pianist with the same years of experience. Yet there is an added dimension to his playing that can only be described as an "extension of his character." His music is filled with love. His playing evokes the peace he has in his own heart. His performance is joyful—his fingers seem to wait patiently in anticipation of the next note. He exudes mercy and kindness through musical expression, and at all moments in the playing, he has control not only over the instrument, but over himself. He plays with a Christ-centered demeanor because He is a Christ-centered person—and at the conclusion of His rendition of the concerto there is a silent awe on the part of his listeners that is very close to the silent awe of worship—not of him, but of the One who has given such a gift and who has made such perfect performance of the gift possible.

Handel attended a performance of his *Messiah* toward the end of his life. During the thunderous standing ovation at the end of the performance, the great composer, by now in a wheelchair, was assisted to the stage. The applause grew even greater as he appeared center stage. Painfully Handel arose and jabbed his cane heavenward. "Thank God, not me," was his message.

All great works are work of the Spirit. The audience had heard a Spirit-inspired performance, a great work of art performed by musicians who were touched by the Spirit as they performed.

The Holy Spirit's love for us becomes the love with which the gifted writer crafts his words, the gifted gardener plans and tends his garden, the gifted painter holds his brush, and the gifted athlete runs his race. The Holy Spirit's joy in us becomes the joy with which the gifted woodworker approaches his next project and the gifted sculptor takes chisel to stone. The Holy Spirit's peace in us becomes the peace felt as the gifted baker kneads his dough and forms his pastries. The Holy Spirit's patience becomes the patience felt as the gifted rug maker ties the thousands of knots that will create a valuable carpet. The Holy Spirit's impartation of kindness and mercy are felt by the gifted designer who seeks for his designs to be a blessing to his clients. The Holy Spirit's gift of self-control is expressed in the beautiful form of balance and coordinated muscle movements displayed by the gifted dancer. It is no less evident in the self-control manifested by the Godly surgeon or physician intent on a lifesaving procedure that requires perfect performance under extraordinary pressure.

These truths about mastery apply to those who function in less "artistic" fields. The counselor, pastor, factory supervisor, preacher, speaker, businessman, dentist, attorney, nurse, metalworker, salesman, fitness expert, auto mechanic—any surrendering person in any job qualifies for the Master's touch. Some of the gifts He blesses are "people abilities." Some are physical abilities related to large and small muscles and sensory perception. Some are mechanical abilities related to the ability to use or manipulate tools and other objects. Some are mental abilities.

All gifts and the resulting skills are subject at all times to the influence of character. And when it comes to character, Jesus is our role model. We are to use our gifts as He desires us to use them. Some people say, "Use your gifts as Jesus would use them if He were walking in your shoes." The truth is, for the believer, Jesus *is* walking in our shoes by the precious gift of His Holy Spirit imparted to us. We are to use our gifts as He leads us to use them! We are to use them to His glory. We are to practice the skills related to our gifts with the Holy Spirit guiding our practice.

How is this possible, however, if we are not fully surrendered to the Lord? Full surrender *must* be in place for us truly to become genuine masters of the gifts given to us. The Holy Spirit cannot flow through us to guide the crafting of our gifts into skills . . . if we are not fully surrendered to the Holy Spirit. The Holy Spirit cannot display mastery of our skills for maximum benefit and effectiveness . . . if we are not fully surrendered to the Holy Spirit.

More than a thousand references in the Old Testament and New Testament testify to God having a plan for each of us. That plan is always tied directly to the gifts God has already placed within us. Surrender puts us into position to truly fulfill this verse of Scripture: "Commit your works to the Lord and your plans will be established" (Proverbs 16:3 NASB).

You Are Fully Gifted

All believers have three types of gifts in their lives. We are each equipped with *natural talents* that may also be considered vocational talents. We are each called by Christ to fill a role of *ministry* in the Church—as a leader or as a layperson, or from time to time as both. We are each called to incorporate *supernatural gifts* in our lives—to be both the giver and receiver of them—and called to manifest the character traits of the Holy One as the Spirit does His counseling, comforting, compelling work within us.

A couple of years after my wife Ginny died, the Lord led me to meet and marry a wonderful woman who was a widow and who lived near my brother—God knew how to put two hurting and lonely hearts together for His purposes in the latter days of both of our lives. The minister who performed the marriage ceremony for my wife Meryl and me was Dr. Ron Williams. Ron has a communication talent—he is adept at both speaking and writing. He is also a skilled organizer of major events. He was called to ministry and as a missionary in Asia, where he worked for more than sixteen years. In addition to administrative duties he performed in the corporate headquarters of his denomination, Ron pastored a Chinese congregation in Los Angeles. He has been used by God in powerful ways and frequently the Holy Spirit uses Him in the spiritual gift of healing. I have personally witnessed people healed in the aftermath of His prayers for them.

In Ron I see a fullness and a balance of God's giftings. His natural talents in speaking, writing, and organizing were blended in a magnificent way with Christ's gift and calling to be a pastor and teacher. He has worked in an area of the world that has experienced great need for healing—not only physical healing but emotional and spiritual healing. Ron is gifted with natural talents that he has developed and that Christ has blended with gifts and the Holy Spirit has empowered with spiritual gifts to create a vessel that is not only filled to overflowing with God's love, but that is very effective in helping others and building up the kingdom of God on this earth.

Ron is a wonderful example to me of this truth: God has a majestic plan for each of us, and collectively for all of us. All that is needed is provided. When a person discovers his gifts, he discovers his special place in God's plan! The Christian life is about servanthood and stewardship. Stewardship of what? Service to whom? We are to be master stewards of our resources, and primarily of our gifts! God gives us our talents, calls us to service, and then empowers us to follow through. In our stewardship of all that He has divinely entrusted to us, we remain His servants. His challenge to us is that if we "invest" or "plant" our talents, then He will multiply what we plant and, in the end, reward us with even more opportunities to plant. We will know His approval and receive His joy.

This was the teaching of Jesus in a parable that He concluded with these ringing words of tribute to the faithful steward and servant: "Well done, good and faithful servant; you were faithful over a few things, I will make you ruler over many things. Enter into the joy of your Lord" (Matthew 25:21 NKJV). At the same time, we find these stinging words of judgment for the one who fails to be a good steward and servant: "You wicked and lazy servant, you knew that I reap where I have not sown, and gather where I have not scattered seed. So you ought to have deposited my money with the bankers, and at my coming I would have received back my own with interest. So take the talent from him, and give it to him who has ten talents" (Matthew 25:26–28 NKJV).

In the Scripture, there are three classes of gifts. Each class comes from one of the persons of our triune God.

Gifts of God, the Father

Through creation God the Father gives each of us the talent to do certain things well, such as writing, mathematics, engineering, marketing, singing, and so forth. The list is endless and continues to change and grow over time. These gifts are distributed randomly, ensuring that all jobs are accomplished and done well, and there will never be any lack in creation.

Because gifts are distributed randomly by our Creator, children rarely have the same gifts as their parents; parents do not have the responsibility or privilege of ascribing gifts to their children. This is important to recognize, not only for parents of children, but also for adult children! The gifts you are given by God the Father are inherent at your birth and are not predicated upon what an influential adult may suggest you are "wise to do" or "should try to become good at doing." Every individual has gifts that can be developed to the level of mastery. *Each of us has the potential to become a master of something.*

In the LifePlanning process, we do a comprehensive "Talent Search" to discern what God has planned for the life of an individual. The surest indicator of vocational calling is one's set of talents. No one is exempt from having talents.

Our talents reveal to us what we are called to "do." Doing flows from being. I like to use the analogy of carpentry tools—a saw is made for sawing, a hammer is made for hammering, a sander is made for sanding, and so forth. In like manner, a musician is made for music, a writer is made for writing, a mathematically gifted person is made for calculating and formulating, and so forth. When a person knows his God-given gifts, he knows what he is supposed to "do" in life.

So many people seem to wonder if they are doing God's will. They wonder about the ideal jobs for them to pursue. A major key to knowing God's will for your life is to determine what He's given you as talents! Your talents are intended for development, for "use"—they are a predictor of what you need to be "doing" and what you are to "be."

Through the years I have been amazed at the number of people who either do not want the gifts they have, or covet the gifts of another person. I have met people who are essentially tone deaf who ardently want to be on stage as a singer. These people may certainly have a talent that could put them onstage—but not as a singer! The person who is dissatisfied with his own gift needs to recognize that in his dissatisfaction, he is also in rebellion before God. God the Father has *made* each one of us with talents expressly designed for a useful slot in the unfolding plan for His creation and His kingdom on this earth. He has designed us specifically to live in a specific time and place, and in that sphere of influence, to use our talents as a means of bringing glory to Him. Know your gifts! Rejoice in them! And develop them—they are your key not only to a career, but to personal fulfillment.

The natural talents given to us by God do not appear in our lives full-blown. We are born with the propensity and potential for development of the gifts—it is our responsibility to develop them through training and use. We must *learn* our gifts, and then practice them faithfully—learning as we practice, and always practicing what we learn. In this way, the gifts grow and develop in us.

Certainly gifts find various avenues of expression according to a person's personality, style, dreams, desires, and affiliations. The core gifts do not change, but they can expand and take on various facets or "shapes" as they are practiced in various settings for various purposes. For example, not all who have musical talent will become instrumental musicians, and not all instrumental musicians will specialize in classical music, and not even all instrumental musicians who specialize in classical music will focus on the old masters or seek to use their musical talents in the context of an orchestra. Without belaboring the play on words, there are many variations on the theme!

In reality, of course, even the talents we have are God's, not ours. They are given in a sacred trust. They are part of God in us. What we do with them is our gift back to God.

Gifts of God, the Son

The gifts of Christ are gifts of ministry. Christ, our "Founding Pastor," gives these gifts to build His church. People are called and equipped to be apostles, prophets, evangelists, missionaries, church planters, church growers, youth pastors, worship leaders, institution leaders, board members, teachers, and so forth. These are special ministries and unique callings.

The gifts of God the Son are revealed to us by direct revelation of Christ. This is what it means to be "called" into ministry for the Lord. Only a believer can hear the Lord's voice calling him to ministry—and only a believer, of course, can fulfill the ministry to which Christ calls the person. A number of pastors through the years have enrolled in the LifePlan process and over the course of our days together, have admitted that they did not feel "called" to the ministry in which they are working. As could readily be predicted, their work was not going well.

I have also encountered people who knew they were called to a particular role in the church, but were resisting that role. One pastor who came to me had been called to ministry at the age of seven. Without any prompting from his parents, he had gone to the altar in his church and had received Jesus as his Savior and committed his life to following Jesus as Lord. He had known almost immediately that Jesus was "calling" him to be a pastor. That particular vocation, however, was not one that either his parents or teachers encouraged. They saw in him a great deal of intellectual ability, and also a love for animals, and they encouraged him to become a veterinarian. When this young man was a junior in veterinary school, God the Son finally said to him, "Enough! You are going to be a pastor." He switched gears dramatically, and today he is a fulfilled, successful pastor, but not a pulpit pastor. His work is his ministry.

There are some who believe that the roles for church leadership are to be found in Ephesians 4:11 (NKJV)—apostle, prophet, evangelist, pastor/teacher. The apostle Paul wrote to the Ephesians that these roles were for the "equipping of the saints for the work of ministry, and for the edifying of the body of Christ, in order to bring the church into unity of faith of the knowledge of the Son of God. Apostles are those who establish new works for the Lord; prophets are those who proclaim the Word of God—with the Good News much more important than prophecy. Evangelists are those who spread the Gospel to those who have not heard it; pastors and teachers are those who nurture and nourish the believers—shepherding them and guiding them into the truth of God's Word by their example and spoken words.

There are others who believe that the listing of ministry gifts in Romans 12:4–8 are gifts of God the Son for all in the church—both those in leadership and the general laity. These gifts were identified by the apostle Paul as being gifts "according to the grace that is given" by Christ and they are to be employed with faith. Specifically, the gifts in this letter of Paul are identified as prophecy (prediction through God's guidance); practical ministry in meeting needs; teaching (of God's Word); exhortation (advising, counseling, giving direction); giving of resources and services; leading or administrating; and showing mercy or hospitality—giving to others in ways that are comforting, encouraging, and uplifting.

The purists believe that Ephesians and Romans cover the entire scope of gifts. I do not believe this for a minute. What I do believe is that God will continue to provide the gifts needed to fulfill His purposes in all periods in history.

The gifts of God the Son are fixed. They do not change over time. They are in consort with the natural gifts given to the person by God the Father, and like our natural gifts, they can be applied and expressed in a tremendous variety of ways. Also like our natural talents, the ministry gifts of God the Son do not appear in our lives full-blown. They must be developed through training and use. A person who is called to a leadership role must learn how to become a good leader, and how to use his giftedness in skilled ways with each new group of believers he encounters during his life. A layperson who recognizes that he has been graced with a gift of generous giving must discern how and when to use that gift for maximum effectiveness. Recently a friend told me about two people she knows who have been given a gift of generous giving. One is a multimillionaire who enjoys giving anonymously to young people who have a desire to attend Bible school but are without funds. The other person is a fairly poor woman who crochets and knits—and who cannot seem to *stop* crocheting baby blankets for even poorer mothers in her community and other communities across her state. She has made and given more than five hundred blankets in the last ten years, mostly from yarn that has been donated to her. The amount of giving is not at question in the giving of the gift or the pursuit of it—it is the impetus deep within the person to "give" that is the grace calling of Christ.

In like manner, the person who is graced by Christ Jesus to be a leader or administrator can't help himself—he will lead the Scout troop, organize the bake sale, sort out the details of a sticky problem, and so forth—not as a burden or chore, but as a natural expression of his call. It is not a burden for such a person to lead. The person graced to fulfill a particular calling of Christ will find great satisfaction in the employment of his gift.

"But," you may be asking, "what about the person who has a talent to sing or construct cabinets?" Those natural gifts will find expression alongside ministry gifts in creative and wonderful ways, and sometimes highly unusual ways. A farmer was once called to be an apostle—he was led by Christ to build a bunkhouse on his farm and to provide a foster home for difficult-to-place teenaged young men. These young men were often on the brink of delinquency or had emotional troubles after years of being in the foster-care system. He gave these young men not only a home, but an opportunity to learn practical skills while working on the farm—everything from shoeing horses to driving tractors. The young men studied for their high-school diplomas in the evenings, and went to church with this farmer and his wife on Sundays. This man had a natural gift for "growing things"—and Christ called him to use that natural gift to "grow young men" who would be useful citizens and followers of Christ. His farm became a model for several others across the nation.

As another example, a young woman gifted to be a musician also had a call of God to teach. She has led children's choirs to national acclaim in both public school settings and church settings—and now she is active internationally using music in some of the poorest areas of the world to teach basic biblical concepts among children and teens.

Natural gifts of God the Father and the grace gifts of God the Son are not one and the same, but they do go hand in glove. A triune God is the giver of both and He is never going to gift us with incompatible gifts—indeed, the blending of natural and grace gifts is nearly always a wonderful expression of God's creativity in our lives.

The Gifts of God, the Holy Spirit

The gifting for ministry is of Christ—the nudging, counseling, and anointing for that ministry are of the Holy Spirit.

Christ's army of the elect build up the church under the Holy Spirit's direction. The whole "Body of Christ" is fitted together perfectly and the Great Commission is completed as an expression of the grace gifts of God the Son, empowered and directed by the spiritual gifts of the Holy Spirit. Each member does his own special work, helping the other members to grow so that the body is healthy, growing, and radiant with love.

The spiritual gifts directly linked to God the Holy Spirit are those that build up the individual believer, and then are manifested through the individual believer for the benefit of the entire body of Christ.

The apostle Paul wrote about specific spiritual gifts to the Corinthians: "Now concerning spiritual gifts, brethren, I do not want you to be unaware . . . Therefore, I make known to you that no one speaking by the Spirit of God says, 'Jesus is accursed'; and no one can say, 'Jesus is Lord,' except by the Holy Spirit. Now there are varieties of gifts, but the same Spirit. . . . But to each one is given the manifestation of the Spirit for the common good. . . . But one and the same Spirit works all these things, distributing to each one individually just as He wills" (1 Corinthians 12:1, 3, 4, 7, 11 NASB).

The apostle Paul was writing to the church in Corinth about the spiritual gifts to teach them about the appropriate use of the gifts in a corporate or "group" setting. The truth that is often overlooked is that Paul also noted that these gifts are given to "each of us." The gifts are resident in the Holy Spirit, anointed with His power, and "distributed"—in combinations and quantities—as He directs. A believer in Christ Jesus has been given the entire Holy Spirit—not a "segment" of the Holy Spirit, but the whole Holy Spirit. The Holy Spirit does not impart only a portion of Himself to a believer, but *all* of His nature. We see this perhaps more clearly in Paul's writings to the Galatians about the fruit of the Spirit. The Spirit creates in us who we are to *be*—loving, joyful, peaceful, patient, kind, virtuous, faithful, gentle, and temperate (see Galatians 5:22–23). These character traits are not *fruits* of the Spirit, but the "fruit." One believer doesn't manifest the character trait of love and another of peace. One believer isn't given three of the nine traits but allowed to remain woefully inadequate in the other six. The nine character traits of the Holy Spirit called "fruit" are intended to be manifested as a whole in a person's life because they are the work of the "whole" Holy Spirit in a person.

In very similar manner, all of the supernatural gifts of the Holy Spirit are resident in the Holy Spirit and they are imparted to us at the time we receive Jesus as Savior, and our surrender to following Him as Lord. They are "available" *to* us for individual spiritual development and for use *through* us to build up the church.

Paul lists nine gifts in his letter to the Corinthians: word of wisdom, word of knowledge, faith, healing, working of miracles, prophecy, discerning of spirits, heavenly language, and interpretation of heavenly language.

In your daily life, you need wisdom! No believer should be without it. We are admonished elsewhere in Scripture to seek it and to ask God for it. *Wisdom is knowing how to apply the truth of God to daily life.* At times, the Holy Spirit will impart to you as an individual a new insight into *how* to live out God's wisdom in your world. At times, the Holy Spirit may impart to you a message related to ways in which your church might manifest God's wisdom to the greater community in which you live.

In your daily life, you need knowledge! We each are exhorted a number of times in Scripture to get knowledge and understanding—we cannot live a holy life in Christ without a knowledge of God's commandments, His promises, His principles and key ideas. We must have a thorough knowledge of God's Word. At times, the Holy Spirit will compel us to recognize something in a new way—perhaps it is a new insight into the meaning of a passage of Scripture, perhaps it is a new insight into the nature of God, perhaps it is a new understanding of what God is doing in a particular area of the world or through a series of events. Sometimes that "word" to us is for our own spiritual growth—sometimes it is given to us to impart to others in the body of Christ so that the entire church group can be strengthened and better prepared for action.

In your daily life, you need faith—there are times when the Holy Spirit will give you faith to believe for something very specific in a way that you have never believed so "strongly" before. You need miracles . . . you need to recognize and be a participant in the working of miracles, which are sovereign and supernatural manifestations of God. A woman once said to me, "When I do something with my will and God adds His power that becomes a true act of willpower. I'm an alcoholic and every day that I determine not to drink, and God adds His power to help me not to drink, is a day that I don't drink. And Brother Paterson, that's a miracle! Ask any alcoholic and he will tell you that every day he doesn't drink is a miracle day."

There are personal and corporate uses for each of the spiritual gifts in 1 Corinthians 12. From personal experience I can assure you that when it comes to the spiritual gifts being manifested in group settings, rarely does a person operate in a spiritual gift *publicly* if that gift isn't already stirring in the person's spirit *privately*. For example, a word of wisdom is nearly always voiced in a public setting by a person who is already immersed in God's Word and is diligently in pursuit of wisdom. The "word of wisdom" gift is manifested in a special way to a group *primarily* as an outgrowth or an "overflowing" of that gift already being manifested in the person's individual spirit. I believe this principle holds true for all of the spiritual gifts listed by Paul.

I facilitated the initial session that kicked off the Saturn car development for my General Motors client. At the end of the day, when the meeting room had cleared out, a senior executive stayed behind to speak to me. He said, "Today I heard the finest Christian witness I ever heard." I was totally unconscious of doing so. He had experienced the public usage of a gifting that I strive to develop privately, first and foremost.

I realize that there are some who theologically believe that these 1 Corinthian 12 gifts are no longer for the church today. Most of those same people, however, will readily admit that every believer should seek to be wise and knowledgeable about the Bible and the nature of God the Father, God the Son, and God the Holy Spirit. They will preach that every believer should seek to grow in faith, pray for healing (of self and others), be open to experiencing miracles, speak out the truth of God to other people, and be able to discern clearly whether good or evil motivations and intents are underlying certain behaviors. The stumbling ground often seems to be with the gifts related to "heavenly language" and its interpretation. I suspect the concern is primarily with the emotional overtones that these two gifts have acquired through the years, rather than with a genuine belief that God not only can but desires to give a unique means of communication to each of His children so that they might praise Him more fully and communicate with Him at greater depth. I have rarely met a surrendered person who did not believe, at his or her core, that God desires to speak directly to the heart of each person, and to reveal Himself to each person in a way that is unique and precious. This happens in prayer. It happens in communication with the Almighty. It happens as we speak and listen. Perhaps when viewed from that simple conceptual foundation, even the gifts of heavenly language and interpretation are not only for each believer today, but also are desirable in the church body as a whole.

Certainly the more a person grows in his relationship with the Holy Spirit, the more he will grow in his understanding of the spiritual gifts of the Holy Spirit. We should always remember Paul's introductory words to these gifts:

- The gifts are diverse but they all flow from the Holy Spirit

- The purposes for the gifts—differences in ministries—may vary from time to time and situation to situation, but the Lord is the one who is working all purposes to His glory and good (see 1 Corinthians 12:4–6).

The gifts of the Holy Spirit are never intended to call attention to an individual. They are intended to build up the whole of Christ's church. Nor are these gifts permanently "fixed" in a person's life as a "role" in the church. There is not one person designated always to be the one with extra faith, another to be the one who is the designated "discerner of spirits." The gifts are distributed in quantity and quality as needs arise and situations change. They are distributed as the Spirit wills.

The Purpose of the Gifts

God's gifts imparted to us—the inherent natural gifts of God the Father, the ministry graces of God the Son, the supernatural gifts of God the Holy Spirit—are given to us for one overriding purpose: to allow us to manifest *fully* the potential God has given to us and the reason for our being on this earth.

You are *meant* to know, develop, and use your grace gifts—and to do so in a way that attracts other people to Jesus Christ and to build up His Body, the Church.

You are *meant* to know the Holy Spirit and to manifest His character traits and be a vessel through which He pours out His gifts—so that you might build up God's kingdom on this earth.

Some questions:

- Are you aware of God's gifts in your life?

- If you are, are you growing in Christ through these gifts?

- Are you ministering to others? (No Christian is exempt from being a minister.)

- Are you aware of roadblocks to your growth?

- If so, what are you doing about them?

- Do you have a strong awareness that *you* have been called by God to be his minister, serving others through your gifts?

If any of your answer to these questions are no, you will find my book on LifePlanning of great help.

We are not today what we were yesterday.
We will not be tomorrow what we are today.
We are in the process of being changed.
It is not the change of mere differences, but a transformation.
We are becoming like Christ.

ETERNITY

LifeGate 7: Sanctified Service

LifeGate 6: Anointing

LifeGate 5: Surrendering

LifeGate 4: Yielding

LifeGate 3: Converting

LifeGate 2: Seeking

LifeGate 1: Awakening

ASLEEP

Seven LifeGates:
The stairway to the transcendent life in the here and now.

chapter 12

Anointed for Loving Service
LifeGate 6

G od's ultimate purpose for us is that we might be set apart as vessels of service—that we might touch others with His love and in His name that they may be healed and made whole. The surrendered soul serves others willingly, not out of duty. Such a person applies the talents he has received from God, who gives distinctive talents to each person in order to equip each person to live a unique life. The person who applies his God-given talents to servanthood is a person who makes a difference in the world. As my friend Bob Buford says, "We move beyond success to significance." The Lord does, however, call and require of you an outpouring of your life in service so that, by the investing of your life substance (talent, gifts, energy, time, and strength), you are "giving" your life for His purposes on this earth.

Through His grace, God gave us His Son to reconcile and restore us to Himself. Jesus not only made reconciliation possible with His death on the cross, but He gave us the example of His earthly life. He is our role model when it comes to service. Jesus not only made possible our birthright to be heirs of God and joint heirs with Himself, but He gently and simply said to all who would accept their birthright, "Follow Me." He extends the choice to follow as just that—a choice. It is not a burden. It is a privilege. It is also the means by which a human being experiences true fulfillment, purpose, and meaning of life. As such, it is the means for exhilarating joy.

God's plan for our lives, positively stated, is for your life and mine to be a witness of His grace. We are to be ministers of His mercy and compassion. The apostle Paul spoke of our service for the Lord in these terms: "Therefore I urge you, brethren, by the mercies of God, to present your bodies a living and holy sacrifice, acceptable to God . . ." (Romans 12:1 NASB). Our standard for life should be to do what Jesus did in His earthly walk—surrender ourselves to be a *living* sacrifice. When we yield ourselves, we are in harmony with God and with the universe. We then have the sum total of reality behind every move we make—we have "cosmic backing." We cannot fail in service that He directs us to do because He is the author and finisher of our work!

Living for Christ may or may not include dying for Christ—as in martyrdom. It most assuredly means dying to self. And to the person who dies to self, the death of the body has little threat. All has already been "sacrificed."

The LifeGate of Anointing

The LifeGate through which the surrendered person moves toward sacrificial service is "Anointing"—a fresh outpouring of the Holy Spirit on the person's life directly aimed at "unleashing" or "releasing" the person's full potential for service.

To anoint is to "install a person into a position of authority." Anointing throughout Scripture involves the application of oil—and oil throughout the Scripture is symbolic of the Holy Spirit. The anointing that the surrendered person experiences is an outpouring of the Holy Spirit into the person's life for the express purpose of "installing" a person as a God-appointed servant, with full authority to release the servant's gifts in some form of ministry to others. In that position of service, the person has tremendous authority in releasing his gifts for ministry. The specific role of service fits the person, and the person fits the service—in both natural and spiritual giftings.

We do not anoint ourselves. We cannot do so. Neither can other people anoint us, *except* as they are directed by the Holy Spirit and function as vessels through whom He works to anoint us. Even so, their efforts are only an outward and visible sign of a work that is inward and invisible, a work performed exclusively by the Holy Spirit. Ultimately, we are anointed by the Spirit and by no other person or means.

A seldom-quoted verse in Deuteronomy says, "You shall have olive trees throughout your territory, but you will not anoint yourself with the oil, for your olives will drop off" (Deuteronomy 28:40 NASB). If we attempt to "anoint ourselves"—setting ourselves up as an authority over an area of service apart from God's Spirit—we will fail. If we rely upon the "good intentions" of other people who seek to install us into positions of spiritual authority without any real impetus or direction by the Holy Spirit, we will also fail. It is the Spirit who anoints, sets aside, purifies, and consecrates us for holy service.

This failure to acknowledge that all *true* anointing comes from the Holy Spirit, and the Spirit alone, is a major reason that many people fail in the performance of their ministries. They are attempting to do something *for* God without the empowerment *from* God for the service they are seeking to render.

In His home town synagogue, Jesus stood and declared, "The Spirit of the Lord is upon Me, because He has *anointed Me* to preach the gospel to the poor; He has sent Me to heal the brokenhearted; to proclaim liberty to the captives and recovery of sight to the blind, to set at liberty those who are oppressed; to proclaim the acceptable year of the Lord" (Luke 4:18–19; Isaiah 61:1–2 NAST).

Jesus was surrendered. He was prepared. He was anointed for a clearly defined mission. His mission was fully released, and He had full authority over it at all times. His three years of ministry changed the world and because he engaged fully in that ministry of ultimate service, He continues to change the world. You and I have the assurance of forgiveness and the promise of life eternal because of Jesus' full surrender to the will of His Father, His anointing by the Spirit, and the fulfillment of His ministry of service.

What the Spirit did for Jesus is available to all who believe in Him, if we are surrendering our lives to Him, and have received the Spirit's anointing for service. The apostle Paul had this advice for his spiritual son, Timothy: "Do not lay hands on anyone too hastily and thus share responsibility for the sins of others; keep yourself free from sin" (1 Timothy 5:22). The anointing for service in the New Testament nearly always involves the application of oil accompanied by prayer and the laying on of hands by spiritual authorities as the Spirit directs. It is just such an act that is referenced in this verse. Paul warned Timothy against engaging in this act of anointing and consecration with undo haste. He cautions strongly against the "sharing" in another person's sins—which is what happens if a person is anointed for service by human agencies prior to the Spirit supernaturally anointing that person. Only the Spirit anoints. Christians tend to be too quick to forgive. It is God who forgives (see Daniel 9:9). 1 Timothy 5:22 points to a critical factor associated with anointing. A sacred vessel is pure. The Spirit anoints those who are righteous—in right standing with God the Father. The Spirit does not anoint those who routinely engage in sin or are impure. To do so would be contradictory—the person could *not* be a sacred vessel for sacred purposes of divine ministry.

Several years ago I had dinner with Sam Moore, who was the chief executive officer of Thomas Nelson publishers at the time. On that occasion, Sam shared that when he was a boy in Lebanon, two Christian missionaries came to the door of his home. They asked if "little Sammy" might attend their school. Sam's mother agreed.

Some years later, Sam left Lebanon to come to the United States. His mother laid hands on him and invoked God's blessing. (In the Middle East it is customary to give one's child a family blessing as the child leaves home.) Once in the United States, this young entrepreneurially bent Christian sold Bibles door-to-door from the trunk of his car. His success at selling Bibles eventually led to his leadership position as the head of one of the largest Christian publishing enterprises in the world. He said to me humbly and matter-of-factly, "To date, I have sold twenty-two million Bibles." Young Christian men and women today help pay their way through college by selling Thomas Nelson Bibles door-to-door during summer breaks. It is a part of Sam's ongoing legacy to the next generation to ensure that God's Word continues to be made available to every person in our nation.

Sam was not only "anointed" by the laying on of hands by his mother, but by the Holy Spirit. His work has prospered in a way that only the Spirit can direct. Even so, Sam's work will remain "unfinished" on this earth. The same is true for all of us. As I have said earlier, only Jesus fully finished anything. Ultimately, it is God who will finish everything. We can, however, *start* something with eternal benefit and ramifications if we yield to God's will and are anointed for His purposes. As God's anointed vessels, we can *begin* a work of service that has no end, but which continues over time and into eternity at the will and empowerment of the One who directs and enables the work. We are *vessels* in His hands.

God's ways cannot be fully analyzed, and frankly, full analysis of God's purposes or methods is none of our business. We can know this: His unlimited love, His gifts, and His grace are freely given. The surrendered person brings praise and worship of the Almighty God, and practical service to others. His loyalty and allegiance are to heaven and as an ambassador of heaven to this earth, his work is to build God's Kingdom as part of the Lord's front-line team.

Anointing Sets Us "Apart"

Anointing sets apart the surrendered saint in a special way for service. To be "set apart" is the essence of sanctification. The word sanctification means "to make sacred, purified." The word in religious circles through the ages has come to mean a "cleansing and setting apart for specified godly service." As perhaps the foremost example, the beautiful gold and silver vessels and utensils in the ancient Jewish temple were sanctified. They were cleansed thoroughly and set apart *only* for use in the Temple. They were kept special for use in worship of the Lord. As set-apart vessels, they were regarded as holy. In a very similar fashion, the believer who is surrendered is cleansed and set apart by the Holy Spirit for God's holy purposes.

Taking people through LifePlans, I have witnessed how God not only has readied, but also has revealed to each person through the process a special work or service. Very often this realization is a "God moment" marked by tears. When it happens, there is no point in proceeding further. Often the person simply needs to be alone with God for a while. I am just as much in awe when this happens as the person experiencing the LifePlan. There is a feeling of divine electricity in the air!

On one occasion a pastor came to my home in Big Bear Lake, California. At that time he served as a consultant and national training director for a major Christian denomination. During the LifePlanning process, we focused on vocational direction. He expressed his hope that he might be named a "supervisor" for this denomination, and specifically that he desired to be named the supervisor over the Pacific Northwest region. Even so, he did not believe that his teenaged children should be relocated. We agreed to pray that night for guidance about this vocational goal he held for his life.

About two o'clock in the morning, the Holy Spirit awoke me and revealed to me that this man was to become the general supervisor of his denomination. This certainly was not a move that was in the normal "flow" of the way things were done. This man had never served as a regional supervisor of any kind, which would have been the normal career path that led upward to the top rung of the ladder.

The next morning, following a brief time of Scripture reading, devotional reading, and prayer, we again invited the Holy Spirit to work in us and through us. I shared what I had experienced during the night. He had received no such message, and frankly he rejected completely the message that I shared with him. He had no belief whatsoever that he would be selected for such a position and most definitely didn't want to relocate to the corporate offices which were far distant.

Within two months, the president of the denomination offered the position of general supervisor to him. He accepted, the family moved, and overall the transition was remarkably easy. Since then, he has been promoted. Fifteen years later, this man is now back in his beloved Pacific Northwest in an administrative capacity with his denomination. The Holy Spirit had only revealed the *next step*—and after years of experience with LifePlanning, I find that is nearly always the case. Rarely is a person given a glimpse into the long-range plan that God has for a person's future when it comes to specific job titles and career roles. The Lord makes it very clear in Scripture the character traits He is seeking to produce in us, and He often makes very clear the overall trend and pattern of what it is He desires for us to accomplish in our lives. I have come to believe that He does *not* speak to us about specific positions or job titles beyond the *next step* because if He did, we would begin to live in the "idea" of that future position or title and fail to do our highest quality work with maximum commitment in the *next step* position.

Sanctified service is the ultimate in self-actualization. One is actualized when she empties herself in service to others. In giving self away, a person acquires life. According to the Maslow model to which I have referred several times, the fully actualized person is a person who is seeking to live up to her mental, emotional, and physical potential. The fully actualized Christian is one who is seeking to grow in spiritual potential through a process of pouring out *self* more and more, and allowing more and more of self to be filled with Christ's presence, ultimately to live this life in the Divine level.

To be a sanctified servant, one must choose a life fully surrendered to Christ and be willing to fully engage in service with his or her giftedness. Self-actualization in the secular sense is a matter of becoming willingly intentional about life. It requires the pursuit only of those things that one knows to be worthy. The same is true for spiritual transformation.

ETERNITY

LifeGate 7: Sanctified Service

LifeGate 6: Anointing

LifeGate 5: Surrendering

LifeGate 4: Yielding

LifeGate 3: Converting

LifeGate 2: Seeking

LifeGate 1: Awakening

ASLEEP

Seven LifeGates:
The stairway to the transcendent life in the here and now.

chapter 13

Sanctified Service

LifeGate 7

T*he person who passes through* the LifeGate of Anointing and enters into Sanctified Service is a person who allows much that is extraneous and without divine purpose to slough away. The focus is totally upon what God desires and what God has willed. The Sanctified Servant is fully conscious of the need to serve, and is intentionally willing to serve in whatever ways the Holy Spirit directs.

Sanctified Service *Is* Your "Calling"

In Christian circles we often hear the phrase, "the calling of the Lord." As previously discussed, the Bible has more than a thousand references to the "calling" of the Lord in a person's life. Sometimes this refers to hearing the voice of the Lord deep within a person's spirit. Sometimes it refers to a particular vocation that a person feels led to pursue. Ultimately, however, the calling of the Lord—the desired work that He plans for each of us to pursue—is to use the talents

God has given us to master something that will build His Kingdom in a significant way.

When you are fully living out your calling of God, you will find that you are bearing these hallmarks:

- You live a life focused on *eternal union*. Eternal union is the free gift of God, offering us an eternal life with our Lord. Sanctification does not earn eternal life; it is God's gracious gift (see Exodus 31:13).

- You rest in *Christ's identity*. To rest in Christ's identity is to be a faithful imitator of Christ.

- You live by the manifold *gifts and graces* of God.

- You live on a *spiritual level*—living in two worlds at once, moment by moment living in and through Christ.

- You *radiate Christ's joy*, lightening the day, giving energy and life to others.

- You are a *blessing* to others.

- You live out the command to *love others*, not causing others to stumble.

- You live out the *truth of Christ*, obeying God's Word because you love Him.

- You earnestly seek to live your life *as Christ did*, empty of self and full of the Holy Spirit.

- You *serve others* and the Lord out of love, not duty.

This last characteristic is the one that I believe lies at the very heart of all callings. What God gifts us to do, He intends for us to do as an expression of His *love*.

As He has gifted us, we are to bless others with our gifts.

As He has loved us, we are to love others.

As we yield ourselves totally to Him, we become His chosen vessels, putting our gifts solely to His glory. His Spirit is co-joined with our spirit. We go beyond our best and cannot fail because we have God supporting our accomplishment of His purpose for our life.

In surrender, we have the exact opposite situation of surrender's normal meaning. We have the ultimate victory through the ultimate partnership.

At the time of this writing I received an email from a man I worked with for many years at Saddleback Church. He was the operating officer for The Purpose Driven Ministry, ultimately accepting a position as chief operating officer for what is now a very large discipleship and teaching ministry. He came to me for a LifePlan and this event led to a moment in which he surrendered to the Spirit. He has led a small start-up organization to three times growth in all key measurements in eighteen months—and during a severe economic downturn.

In discussing his moment of surrender he writes, "I've never been the same since. I certainly wouldn't have been the management leader for The Purpose Driven Life if we hadn't had that moment. There are only a handful of people who have had such a significant impact on my life—and you probably didn't know you did at all. I'm not the most famous, nor have I written books that have sold tens of millions, but my hands do impact over eight hundred thousand souls per week now, and what I've learned as a leader and manager can be significantly attributed to your tutelage. So, thank you!" A life which is a new life in Christ, teamed with the Spirit. A life which cannot fail. A victorious life in and through Christ. Thank you, God.

God showers His surrendered children with His awesome love. Through its power they are transformed into His likeness. They assume the mind of Christ. They become Everyday Saints. Their touch, physically or verbally, heals.

Love is a priceless possession. It is the most powerful force in the world. If love were totally harnessed, it would be a force greater than the winds, the tides, electricity, or atomic power. The transcendent love of Christ becomes ours when we yield to Him totally, gifting our Lord with all that we are and all that we can become, and receiving in return His greatest gift, His loving presence.

Once we have received God's love into our lives, its power enables us to live fully for Him. We find that we have but one purpose: to serve Him here and in eternity. The more we experience the fullness of God's love, the more full our life becomes. We find ourselves both eager and able to live out His promise to us of a joyous life of service as we engage in the tasks of building His Kingdom.

The Command to Love

The bestowing of God's love on us is always followed by God's command that we bestow that love on others.

A Pharisee, an expert in the Law, attempted to trap Jesus in a legal argument one day by asking Him the most important commandment to fulfill. "Teacher, which is the great commandment in the Law [of Moses]?"

Jesus replied—not by telling him the "most important" commandment but by saying, *"You shall love the Lord your God with all your heart, and with all your soul, and with all your mind.* This is the great and foremost commandment. And a second is like it, *'You shall love your neighbor as yourself'* " (Matthew 22:37–40 NASB).

The truth is, if we truly love God with our whole heart, soul, and mind, we *will* seek to keep all of God's other commandments. We will *want* to keep the Ten Commandments, and all of the other "thou shalt" commands of God throughout His Word. If we truly love God, we will *want* to love what God created and what God loves—very specifically, ourselves and other people. We will fall in love with God anew or for the first time: we will live in sanctifying moments. "Thy will be done"—Jesus, on the cross; Mary, when the angel asked her to birth our Savior; Paul, when he was converted. We do morally good acts out of love, not duty. Every day is filled with our doings, small and large acts. If done with great love for our Lord, He smiles. They are noble and Holy acts.

Our experience with His love gives us the faith to trust Him, obey Him, and seek Him continually. And when we fail in our trust, our obedience, or our seeking . . . He instantly convicts us and brings us again to repentance. We have an awareness of what we have done and left undone in loving Him, trusting Him, obeying Him, and seeking Him. We have a desire to yield once again, and as we do, we experience yet another outpouring of His pure and unconditional love.

I'll give you a personal story. As a young husband, I'd gag if I changed a baby's diaper. So, I didn't do it. When my wife Ginny was ill with lung cancer, she became progressively less able to care for herself. Finally, she could do nothing for herself; could not turn in bed, lift an arm, feed herself. She was ill for thirty-nine months, totally unable to take care of herself over the last year. I had her at home in our bedroom. I installed a stair lift so she could be put in a wheelchair and get downstairs or outside. On the weekends and at night, I was the nurse. God gave me the love to take care of her needs, whatever they were: toilet, food, medicine. I became fiercely protective. I felt it my honor to live out "in sickness and in health"—from the wedding vow fifty-four years earlier.

The Spirit enables us to fulfill and keep God's commandments. The plain and simple reality is that we cannot keep God's commandments totally by our own willpower. We are weak. We don't do what we want to do. We do what we don't want to do. That's not just reality for some of us—it's reality for every human being. The Spirit knows this. He *empowers* us with love. He *empowers* us to keep His commands to love.

Let me emphasize the point that God does not "suggest" that we love. *He commands that we love. We are to love God. We are to love ourselves. We are to love others in the same way we love ourselves. God has graced us with the predisposition to love.*

"But," you may say, "how can it be true love if God *commands* us to love Him?"

He commands our love—our full devotion, our total yielding to Him—because He knows that in loving Him, we will be in a position to receive all that we desire, and all that is for our eternal good. He commands us to love because in opening our hearts, souls, and minds to God, we are opening the door to receiving the outpouring of His love into every area of our lives. It's as if we are opening a door to let something "out," and in so doing, we create the means by which everything for our benefit can come flooding in. Because we are created in God's image we have a free will to choose. It's our choice to live for Him or to not do so. It was for our freedom that Christ set us free (see Galatians 5:1).

The *degree* to which we love depends on how much we surrender. We are to love God with *all* our heart, with *all* our soul, and with *all* our mind. All is all. Nothing is held back. Nothing is taken off the table. Nothing is allowed for self-consumption or self-direction.

To love fully—to give the full devotion of our heart, soul, and mind—is to be in a position to receive God's love fully. How He delights in loving us that way! How He delights in filling us up to the overflow point with His acceptance, affection, value, worth, and presence!

I have stood on the cliffs of Normandy which one thousand Rangers scaled in World War II. They are straight up. Only sixteen got to the top, the rest were killed by machine guns. They were after the Germans' big guns and found them already removed. Jesus said, "Greater love has no one than this, that one lay his life down for his friends" (John 15:13 NASB).

I was in the Fifth Marine Division. It was the lead division which took Iwo Jima. We had a very large division of 33,000. Iwo Jima cost 5,931 dead (19 percent) and 17,272 wounded (52 percent), for a total of 71 percent casualties. I received a medical discharge just prior to the campaign. I know that many readers of this book weren't even alive when World War II took place, but I feel compelled to share this bit of history. The Royal Air Force, which saved England, had 94 percent casualties at the end of the "Battle for Britain," which led Winston Churchill to say, "Never in the course of history have so many owed so much to so few."

We owe our lives to a few, and our eternal lives to One. What should our response be to such a lavish, infinite outpouring of God's love into our hearts? It is praise and thanksgiving. It is an opening of ourselves more and more to give love.

We yield to God's love fully. We acknowledge His love fully. We receive it, embrace it, cling to it with all that we are and have. We delight in it, wallow in it, and rejoice in it. We cry out, "More! I yield more! I submit more! Pour into me *more* of Your love!"

And God does.

We are in free fall. We can't get enough time with the One we love. We are compelled to touch. I never felt more holy with Ginny than when we were being intimate. It never changed. When our children came along we had no favorites. God enlarged our hearts each time. If He hadn't done this, there would have been a tendency to either give less love to each child or have favorites. Our Christian faith is unique among religions with respect to its focus on love and God's love for each of us. *When God's power infuses our will it results in hope and love. When it infuses our intellect we believe in Him. This is how God has provided for us to believe in Him, know Him, and love Him.*

The surrendered soul radiates God's love unconditionally to all he encounters. He becomes a shining light in a dark world. The love of God, fully received and then fully given, causes others to say, "If that's what it means to be a Christian, I want to be one." The witness of love speaks for itself. Lives lived fully in God's love speak louder than volumes of sermons. Few things irk me more than to witness a "tired love"—an older couple in a restaurant not talking, the husband reading his newspaper. When I see a couple obviously enjoying each other, I often go over to them and tell them how much I appreciate their example, their witness.

God's love also equips us for the eternal life. The more we experience God's love flowing in us and through us during this earthly journey, the more clearly we have a glimpse of what is in store for us when we go "home" to spend eternity with our Lord. We live in the "now, and the not yet" simultaneously. We experience the fullness of his love in earthly vessels, knowing that there is a vastness to His love that we will only experience when we slip the bonds of time and space and dwell eternally in His near presence.

A Position on God's A-Team

Loving, sanctified service puts you on God's A-Team.

God is the Highest Power, the highest of the high. All supreme leaders, in corporations, government, and the military have other leaders who serve under them. The same is true in the spiritual realm. God, the Highest Power—one often referred to in Scripture as the Almighty—appoints people to leadership positions under him.

God's A-Team is the elect, those who are surrendered, sanctified servants. They are the prime movers of His kingdom. They may not be recognized by the world as leaders. Their positions of service may not be of great public note. Their family may not be "distinguished" and may not even have much social status. Nevertheless, they are Kingdom builders because they have come to surrender and have been clothed with "power from on high." God ordains them and installs them into leadership. It isn't a choice of man. God will have His way with the surrendered soul, just as He did with Paul. The choice for leadership is His.

The Word of God is filled with examples of leaders who were chosen by God for unique tasks in the development of his Kingdom. Jesus, of course, is the ultimate example. Sent from heaven rather than called from earth, Jesus nevertheless faced the challenge of surrendering His humanity to the Father.

One of the longtime personal assistants of Kathryn Kuhlman, Dr. Dick Scott, once told me an interesting story. Kathryn Kuhlman was one of the most noted people involved in a healing ministry from the 1940s through the 1960s. Dick was her assistant for nearly twenty years and became a leader in the Foursquare Church. Before every public healing service she held, Kathryn prayed earnestly, "Lord, if You are not with me tonight, I'm not going out there." She simply would not move from her backstage dressing room until she had full assurance in her heart that the Lord was requiring her to preach and proclaim God's healing power to the people. Until she felt the Lord's presence with her, she did not budge.

Kathryn Kuhlman knew that she did not possess personal power in herself to heal. She also knew that she was hooked up to an infinite Power Source—the phenomenal results in her ministry confirm that as the Spirit worked *through* her. Oh, those that each would be as wise in the execution of the sanctified service to which they are called!

The simple truth is this: *There is no higher purpose for your life than to use the fullness of the gifts God has given you in loving service to others. That is the essence of fulfillment. It is the reason for your life and mine.*

chapter 14

Where Are You?

Does Jesus have lordship over *all* of *you*? Jesus said, "I want all of you; your heart, mind, and soul."

The heart is regarded as the seat of our emotions. Paul writes in Romans 10:10 (NAST): ". . . for with the heart man believes, resulting in righteousness, and with the mouth he confesses, resulting in salvation . . ." (a virtuous life). When we yield only our minds we have yielded only part of us. This is the major void in the church. Until we yield our hearts we are not fully committed Christians. And, as I said earlier, surrender requires both intellectual and emotional readiness.

Here's a process which will help you no matter where you are in the path to the transcendent life, to life on the Divine level:

NATURE OF COMMITMENT

	Intellectual (Mind)	Emotional (Heart)

God gave us the ability to rationalize—to reason, think things through.

I COULD propose to that wonderful girl. We enjoy each other.
I SHOULD propose to her. I have courted her for a year. We know each other well.
I CAN marry her. She will accept my proposal.

All these are of our mind—and just as God intended. But they are not commitments.

We fall in love when the heart takes over. *I cannot get enough of this wonderful girl. I want her forever. This is true love, not infatuation.* What becomes transformational love is when the mind combines with the heart in an "I will" statement. *I will be a dedicated husband. I will love and cherish you forever. I will care for you in sickness and in health.*

Where are you with regard to Jesus? Be honest. Are you in love with Him? Do you serve Him out of love or duty? Place yourself on this "Could/Should/Can/Will" scale. Only if you are truthful with yourself will this process be of real help. It is foolish to fool others;

it is criminal to fool yourself. There is no right or wrong on this test. The truth is what matters here. Where are you? . . . Just between you and me.

Only the fully committed accomplish anything. Millions of Christians lead a half life, a counterfeit life, never knowing the deeper, richer, fuller life of a soul centered on Jesus, because they are not fully committed believers.

The "I will" cannot be forced, but you can, through prayer, faith, and self-knowledge, manage your walk. Appendix 1 has a list of prompts which can help you consider how you might ask God to lead you in growth. A LifePlan professionally facilitated by one of our credentialed associates may be in order. My book *Living the Life You Were Meant to Live,* can be a great help. For information on either, see page 243.

If you are ready to surrender, my Surrender Prayer will help you cross over. It has helped many people, some of whom have framed it and resurrender each day. I can testify to the effectiveness of praying daily for a life centered on our Lord.

I commend you to set time aside for meditation each day. You might focus solely on those attributes of Jesus that you wish to become a part of your personality, changing focus with each day of the week (for review, see pages 166–67). Each year you might develop a new list of seven attributes of our Lord that you wish to make "you." *Without any special effort, just the focus, you will become the person you are praying to become. It's not work; it's the power of His love. Remember, His yoke is light.*

Paul's surrender made him the Great Apostle. Only God knows the specifics of what your surrender will lead to. We do not need to know. What we can be certain of, however, is that our life will be lived to His Purpose, His Glory, and that the Kingdom will be advanced, if we forever endeavor to seek out what it means to live a deeper, richer, fuller spiritual life, each and every day.

Prayer of Surrender

Lord,

You know the entire course of my life, as the Author, Perfector, and Finisher of my fate. You knew me before my conception. I was created by You and born to be free and truly alive. Such a life, however, is not what I have led. I have not been in phase or in alignment with Your will. I know that You are the Way. You have shown me Your path of life.

I want to walk humbly beside You, now and forever. I want to live my life within Your will. I may not always do so—even when I believe I am doing so, I may not be. But, Lord, You know my heart. You will not let me stray.

I am safe in Your love and my heart is to please You. You are my all. I have but one overriding goal: to glorify You, Father. I want to please You with the life I lead for You. Your Word has instructed me in how to live in accord with Your will. Help me to live out Your Word in this world.

Thank you, Father, that You are bringing me to heaven: I am on the path! Thank You for giving me a glimpse of heaven every day I am here. Thank You, Father, for Your fullness of life, full measure, tamped down yet overflowing.

Because I have surrendered, You now live—REALLY LIVE—within me. My heart has infinitely enlarged its capacity to love. I am becoming a reflection of You. I am serving You through my talents. I am crafting them, becoming their master. My life now has great purpose, my mission is clear. I am free, radiantly alive. I look forward to each day of your grace.

Bless you, Father. Amen.

_____   _____

Signed   Date

The apostle Paul led a life defined by a passion for Christ.
He lived God's Law of Love.
He rejoiced in God in all circumstances.
He counted every trial as nothing, for
the privilege of being with God in glory.
Likewise, may my faith become a Paul-like faith,
overcoming whatever may happen to me.
May I come into the freedom of
absolute surrender.

Afterword

Tom Paterson writes that God's dream for him, "to sense, receive, and share God's love in every hour of his life," is also God's dream for you. Throughout this book Tom has guided you toward this dream by helping identify where you are in your walk of faith and how to move on to the next LifeGate.

I met Tom in September 1993 when he facilitated my LifePlan at Big Bear, California. For the nearly twenty years since, I have had the privilege of knowing Tom and walking with him through some of the pain and loss described in this book. Although we are now separated by geography, we talk often by phone, and it is my observation that Tom's process of personal surrender is indeed a pivotal point in his life. My visits with Tom, whether in person or by phone, resonate with his process of surrender. He has achieved the peace and unity he describes in this book.

One way he has done that is through spending time with God. Tom's desire for each of us is that God's values become our values. A close personal relationship with God can develop when we're talking with Him. However, we cannot hear God's voice if we're doing all the talking. It is necessary for us to take time to listen to God. Tom indicates that if he had one wish for every reader of this book, it would be that each reader would invest one hour every day in solitary meditation.

Tom talks a lot about process because he is a process person. By that I mean he thinks strategically, gathers data, analyzes it, and follows a process to come to a conclusion and develop a plan—be it a LifePlan or a strategic plan—for an individual, a church, or a company. "The process of transformation and transcendence is never complete," Tom says. "It continues throughout eternity. . . . I truly do not know anything more exhilarating than to live a surrendered life of anointed and loving service. This *is* the life we were meant to live!"

Tom recommends looking for our own wise counselors—I am fortunate to have found a wise mentor in Tom, and I have come to appreciate and love him. "Perfect practice makes perfect," Tom says. I believe this book provides an excellent process to follow for a fulfilled life. Tom's work deserves your careful and prayerful consideration as you pursue a *Deeper, Richer, Fuller* life.

—Jim Buick, former president and CEO
of Zondervan Corporation

About LifePlanning

For information on the LifePlanning process and/or a facilitator near you, call or write:

Pete Richardson
Executive in Charge
LifePlanning, North America Operations
406 E. Baseline Road
Lafayette, CO 80026
(720) 289-7061
or visit his website: pete.richardson@mac.com

You can get my book *Living the Life You Were Meant to Live* by emailing me at tompaterson3925@msn.com.

The LifePlan Process

Tom Paterson is a renowned business strategist and management consultant who has assisted many businessmen in answering questions of perspective, priorities, and purpose in their lives. His reach does not stop in the corporate world, however; Tom has also worked with church leaders to help them discover the course that their lives are meant to take.

Through this, Tom has developed his LifePlan process. In *Deeper, Richer, Fuller*, Tom takes us through the steps of his process and wills us to enter into a deep and meaningful friendship with God. *Deeper, Richer, Fuller* is meant to open our souls and transform our lives by pointing readers toward the ultimate goal of life in Christ: joyful and fulfilling service that radiates God's love to others.

Tom provides us with stories, exercises, and examples of how to strengthen our friendship with God. It is through this that we can begin to lead deeper, richer, and fuller lives.

Discussion Questions

1. What kind of Christian does Tom Paterson admit he was for nearly twenty years? What event caused him to "wake up" to the fact that he was "asleep"? What was the outcome of the event, and why do you think it served to strengthen his faith?

2. Entering into a friendship with God is one of the end goals of *Deeper, Richer, Fuller*. What does a divine friendship with Him entail, exactly? Is it forced? Do you agree with Paterson's notion that "friendship is rooted in religion"?

3. Paterson remarks that we are "creatures bound in time and we develop over time." What is it about being bound in time that can make it difficult for us to develop our friendship with God?

4. How does Paterson think most people view the spiritual world? How does he think we *should* view it? How did Jesus think we should view it? Which viewpoint do you agree with and why?

5. Throughout *Deeper, Richer, Fuller,* Paterson points out the importance of perspective and how it relates to our growing relationship with God. How do we go about making our perspective clear? Where does the concept of H.O.W. fit into this?

6. Talk about LifeGates. Where do they fall on the pathway of our lives? Why does Paterson think we need to be concerned with them? How do they work to improve our relationship with God?

7. Paterson outlines the seven stages of transcendence and describes the effects of each stage. Do you agree with his summations? Why or why not? Do you think there should be more steps? Fewer?

8. What is an Everyday Saint? What are the three steps to becoming an Everyday Saint? How did Paterson initially learn these steps?

9. Discuss the concept of salvation and its importance in *Deeper, Richer, Fuller*. What are the ways in which we can be saved from sin? What is the importance of salvation?

10. Talk about the three abilities that the Holy Spirit imparts upon us. What is the importance of each? How must we utilize them as we journey through the LifeGates?

11. Do you agree that in order to get the most out of our spiritual lives we must surrender ourselves to God? Is it possible to incorporate the lessons learned in this book and live a faithful life and not surrender?

Author Questionnaire

1. What was the inspiration for putting all your thoughts on paper? Why do you think a book like *Deeper, Richer, Fuller* is needed now more than ever?

In my first book, *Living the Life You Were Meant to Live,* I had two chapters on surrender. My editor said I was overpowering my book with surrender and asked that I take one chapter out and save it for the next book. I did that and put it in this book without change. Surrender is the great near void in the Christian church. Have you ever even heard a pastor give a sermon on the subject? Fulton Sheen went so far as to say that Christianity does not become so until one enters the mystical stage through surrender. Surrender is the path to a life as an Everyday Saint. Europe has now gone secular and we are moving in that direction.

2. The concept of the eight stages of transcendence is a cornerstone of *Deeper, Richer, Fuller.* Is it ever possible to get "stuck" in one stage? How can people take the next faith-filled step to the next stage?

One can get stuck in a stage. Most Christians are. One can regress. With so many, many millions of people losing their homes due to unemployment there has been a sliding backward to insecurity. When you place yourself in God's hands, taking the next step is easy. Repeatedly in the Bible our Lord tells us to "only believe." He wants a total belief . . . he wants all of us, our heart, our mind, our soul . . . ALL. ALL is ALL.

3. You openly admit that the loss of three of your four children was a heartbreaking experience, yet it served to strengthen your relationship with God. What advice would you give to a parent who has just lost a child? How can they continue to work to strengthen their friendship with God despite such a tragedy?

Over 80 percent of marriages fail after the loss of a child. The grief is mirrored in your partner's eyes. Unless we have surrendered, the agony is just too much and the marriage fails. My wife and I pulled together. Our love for each other was ever more intense throughout our marriage. We lost two of our four children when Ginny was alive. Our son, Jim, was killed after Ginny died. I am glad she didn't have to live through that. They are all together now in heaven, and because there is no time in heaven, we will be together again in a moment from their perspective.

4. Many people only hear the "good news" when they are seeking forgiveness. Is it possible to hear the good news in a time of happiness? If we have happiness, have we already heard the good news?

There is a strong tendency to turn to God when we are in trouble and to forget Him when happy. When we have yielded to our Lord completely, we are bathed in His light . . . we see the world as for the first time . . . in Technicolor. I start every day thanking him for the wonderful world I live in. Surrendered Christians live in two worlds at once: They live the Good News.

5. Why do you think people resist becoming Everyday Saints? What holds them back? What would you say to someone struggling with the notion of becoming an Everyday Saint?

We resist becoming Everyday Saints because we see it as having to give up the little avarices we are enjoying. Deprivation. Augustine's mother prayed for her son for over twenty years. He kept telling her, "I want to be good but later. I am having too good a time." She asked God if she could stop praying for her son. God told her to continue praying for him. This is the person who became St. Augustine, one of the greatest Christians the world has ever produced. Our finite minds cannot understand the infinite. I don't waste a second trying to understand why it took more than twenty years to give the world Augustine.

6. *Deeper, Richer, Fuller* combines the elements of an advice book with a daily workbook. Was there ever any inclination to lean more in one direction than the other?

Yes, there is a tendency for our day and its pressures to crowd time with God out. I have done more LifePlans with pastors than anyone else in the world at this point. We start the day with a devotion. Pastors who are at my home always join in gladly. Not one has said they have a devotion at home. They tell me that they do not do so.

7. Surrender is a large part of a successful conversion. And yet you emphasize the importance of passion for our talents and how we need to better ourselves. How can someone be sure they are not leaning too much in one direction? Can we surrender "too much" or be "overly" passionate?

We can avoid leaning in one direction too much by assessing how we are investing our time. I think of time in terms of an investment: I don't "spend" time. I am working on the amount of time I invest in meditation. It is too little. I underinvest at this time in it.

8. Is it possible for this book to function as advice on how to become a better person? That is, can someone utilize this book to inspire better relationships with their friends, their family, and themselves (if not God)?

This book will result in better relationships with everyone if the path to transcendence is lived out. In fact, the original name I had for this book was *Becoming Best Friends with God*. I have a covenant with God that every word I speak to another person will be a blessing, never a curse. I will not tell a joke that is at someone's expense . . . as most "Polish" jokes are. I will not let a grandchild tell one. I politely tell them not to tell such jokes and I tell them why. Such stories are curses.

9. What's next for you?

I have a forty-page outline of a book I call *Parenting in Christ: Helping Your Children to Live the Life They Were Meant to Live*. God didn't want that book to be next. He wanted *Deeper, Richer, Fuller*. I could not write another word after I finished the outline. When I got back to His work, the words just flowed. I think it is time for the parenting book, but I have not been nudged to do it at this point. God sets my agenda.

Enhancing Your Book Club

The author recounts several stories of "alarm moments," where he heard, saw, or felt God reach out to him to give advice and inspiration. Has this ever happened to you? Share such a moment with your book club!

Give an honest evaluation of yourself and find out which stage of transcendence you are at. Are you sleeping? Awakening? Seeking? If you'd like, share your results with your book club!

Have a favorite passage from the Bible? Share its meaning and importance to you with your book club.

About the Author

Tom Paterson is a sought-after business strategist, management consultant, and world-renowned inventor whose work has left a lasting mark on our nation and the world, at a level that few individuals in history have accomplished. He has walked alongside four U.S. presidents and some of the greatest business leaders of our generation. In addition, he has sparked the invention of countless products, systems, and services that have made an impact on the very fabric of our society today. In addition, many CEOs, pastors, and other leaders have applied Paterson's strategic insights at a personal level, restructuring their own lives around their unique purpose through Paterson's LifePlan Process.